Seeing Life Through Different Lenses

Ashling McGee

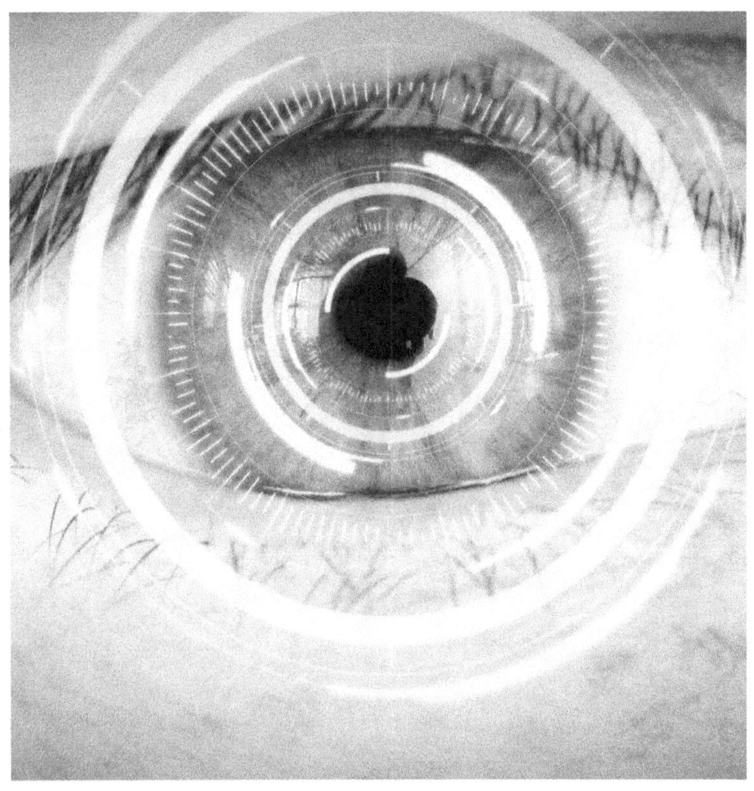

This book is a perspective on how life can be seen through different lenses. Everyone has their perspective on life. This is just opening the mind to a different viewpoint on how one might see it and judge it—giving food for thought on how it has changed or not changed throughout history to the present and what the future may hold if things change or not.

<u>Introduction</u>

This book is a collection of different lenses through which one can see life unfolding. It shows the past, present, and future. From the start, humankind has tried to separate itself from the natural world. As humans, we are responsible for looking after the world and everything in it, but humans started taking advantage of the earth for greed, taking more than they needed. This leads to jealousy, poverty, wealth, and trying to outdo one another to show who is best. We all are the same sinners and saints, but some fall victim to sin as greed takes hold, the need for more and not seeing the consequences of what it leaves behind. This did not start from the present but at the beginning of time. Is this the world we live in, and is this the world we want the next generation to live in? Can it be changed? Is it too late? Have we all destroyed what matters and fallen out of harmony with nature and working as one?

The most extensive present form of life is how we use social media. It can be a great tool and a form of destroying lives if you let it. Social media is used in so many different ways, and it should be used to give a positive outlook and help others love themselves as individuals. To stand proud of the person you are and just be yourself. Filters are great, but they take away from the real you and show how you look at yourself. If you look at yourself unfiltered and see the true you, you are on the way to being your best version. Everyone strives to be a better version of themselves, and if you share that with others, it impacts their lives. Anyone can post a selfie and look happy, but are they pleased, or is it just a lens to disguise their true self as they may feel insecure and going through hell but do not want to show it to the world? Generations have demonstrated how different lenses define a person and how humanity finds its way. The saying " a picture paints a thousand words" leaves an impression and a different meaning for each individual.

Throughout the book, the past, present, and future show how we see life. It unfolds and gives excellent insight into how others were judged and mistreated in many forms. This is still happening in today's society. The book is shown through a combination of a Social Media lens, a self-perception lens, a literature lens, a history lens and a photo and poetry lens. Looking at the past, has the future changed? Well, I will leave that up to you, the readers. This is just one person's view and insight on life through different lenses. It shows how one sees life unfolding and how it has or has not changed throughout history. It also indicates oneself as an individual. Is life moving forward, or are we still living in the past in some ways regarding ideals, tradition and how we were raised as children? Can one change their point of view and learn new ways of living, or are some still influenced by tradition and the old way of living? It is like the saying 'you cannot teach an old dog new tricks'. Is this true in modern society, or can we be

taught new ideals?

<u>Contents</u>   **Page**

Social Media

And

Self-perception Lens

This section is about social media and Self – Perception Lens. Nowadays, everyone turns to social media and has accounts, but are we getting drawn into the propaganda of these media accounts? Have the younger generation, even the older generation, been influenced by what they see and read on these accounts, which can lead to self-destruction of someone's mental health? When you think of it, social media has become more advanced in technology. You read the newspaper or watch adverts on television or certain shows, and they, in some ways, influence how our minds think of things or how we look or dress. Wanting the new styles in fashion, hair accessories, etc., in today's world has not changed as now there is more out there in terms of social media that can determine how you see yourself and create doubt that you are not good enough or you have to do this or that to succeed. It influences how one thinks and follows specific trends and can positively and negatively affect people. It is a good platform for getting your voice heard on certain ideals and things you feel strongly about, but can it turn the opposite way in that it makes others follow because of the trend, or is everyone else doing it, and why should I be left out? It is swaying a person to follow without thinking about it first and if it is what they want or just following along. It is conflicting; some can become submissive and might not be as strong-willed or self-confident as others. Tearing down someone's self-confidence can be quickly done by those on social media, which is wrong and horrible. It happens daily, but if we look at the past, we can easily see that this has also happened. Have things changed? Is the world getting better, or is it getting worse? That is the question one must ask oneself: how can they improve and make a better future for the next generation?

<u>Never Judge a Book by Its Cover</u>

Some images with sayings can inspire people or give them a view of their characteristics, vulnerabilities, and preferences, and they should not be seen as first impressions only.

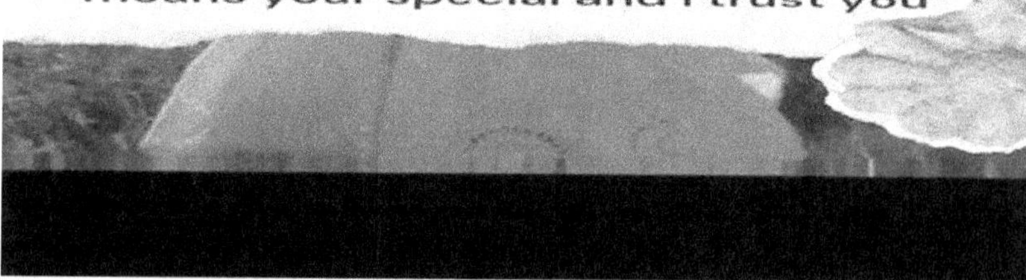

Seeing Life Through Different Lenses
Ashling McGee

<u>You Hold the Key</u>

We all have days that feel like hell on earth. We have good and bad days, and we struggle like everyone. We move forward little by little. One thing to remember: you hold the key to unlocking your happiness. You can turn the key anytime. You must be ready and robust but have the power and strength to turn that key into your desired happiness. It begins and ends with you. It always has and will always be there within you. Just believe and turn the key to unlock what you have been waiting for.

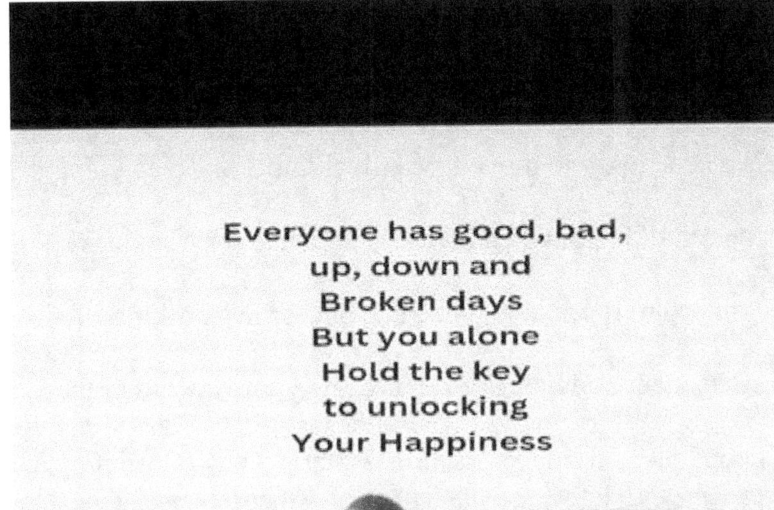
Everyone has good, bad,
up, down and
Broken days
But you alone
Hold the key
to unlocking
Your Happiness

<u>Move Forward in Life</u>

Sometimes, we get bogged down with the past in our heads. We need to try to move forward with life and keep going instead of looking behind us. Your hands are what make you begin. It can be by reaching out for help, asking someone for advice, or even digging your way out of the deep hole you find yourself in. It starts with you wanting to move forward and live and not living in the past. Yes, we have memories, good and bad, but they do not define our future. They are just memories and need to be kept there, not stuck in our minds, constantly stopping us from moving forward. Look back, yes, of course, and remember, but do not stay in the past as that is where it should stay, no you. It would be best to move towards the future, build new memories, live in the now, and see what the future would bring.

Sometimes your head
Is clouded with the past ...

Just remember
Your hands hold
the future

<u>Choose Life</u>

life has its ups and downs, but do not sit around and wait for Life to come to you. You are responsible for making life happen, so be happy now and in the present. You will miss out if you do not take chances and make life happen for you. Time goes by quickly, and the days turn into years when you let it slip away. Be bold. Do what makes you happy and live to the fullest, even when complicated. Life can be messy, but that is what life and living are. Do not sit on the sidelines. Just be BOLD and go for it.

Here is some food for thought on how to live life as a person and an individual.

These two quotes are stimulating

"I exist as I am. That is enough" (Walt Whitman)

"I dwell in possibility" (Emily Dickinson)

Seeing Life Through Different Lenses
Ashling McGee

<u>Seasons Change</u>

Seasons come and seasons go; life is similar, and we change and grow. Do not let time slip away, and hide yourself from being yourself. You are unique, so do not be ashamed and let others tear you down for being a wonderful part of this world and sharing it with everyone.

<u>Self – Perception through media</u>

These are images with words to empower others and give them food for thought as they live their lives. Positive words can help many, and words can mean different things to different people. It is how you see them and how you interpret them.

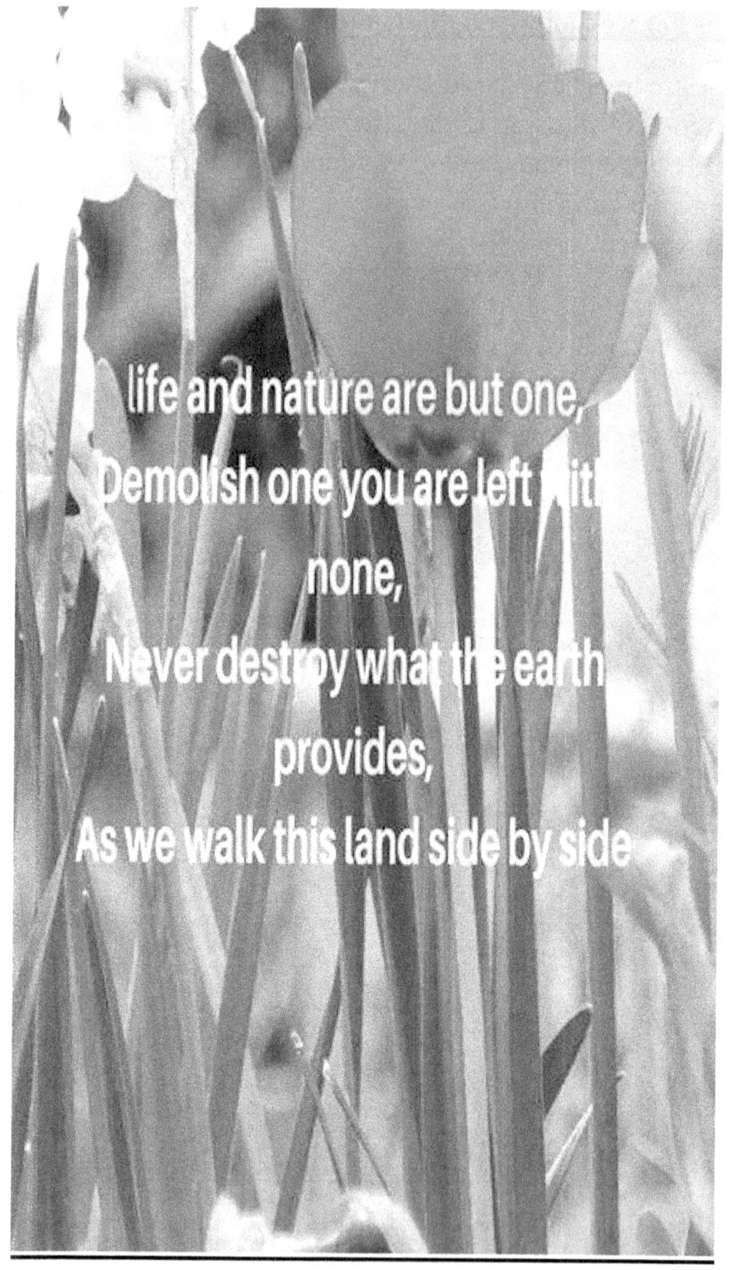
life and nature are but one,
Demolish one you are left with
none,
Never destroy what the earth
provides,
As we walk this land side by side

Always look up its a great big sky,
May feel alone but give it time,
As trees grow tall your strength will too,
Day by day believe in you,

<u>You are Strong</u>

Look at the wonder and the world around you. Open yourself up to the possibilities and share yourself with everyone. Show your true self, and never be ashamed of who or what you are. You are special.

we are all stronger than we
believe,
But Time keeps moving,
We need to stop sometimes
and just breath

Sometimes the calm can revibe
the mind,
Breathe search for clarity and you
may find,
peace within yourself and a fresh
new look,
Just stopping and breathing is all
it took.

Roads lead us down different paths
Never be afraid to walk it alone

Seeing Life Through Different Lenses
Ashling McGee

Take the time to enjoy the things you love
Life is for living so go live it
Don't dream it just live it

Seeing Life Through Different Lenses
Ashling McGee

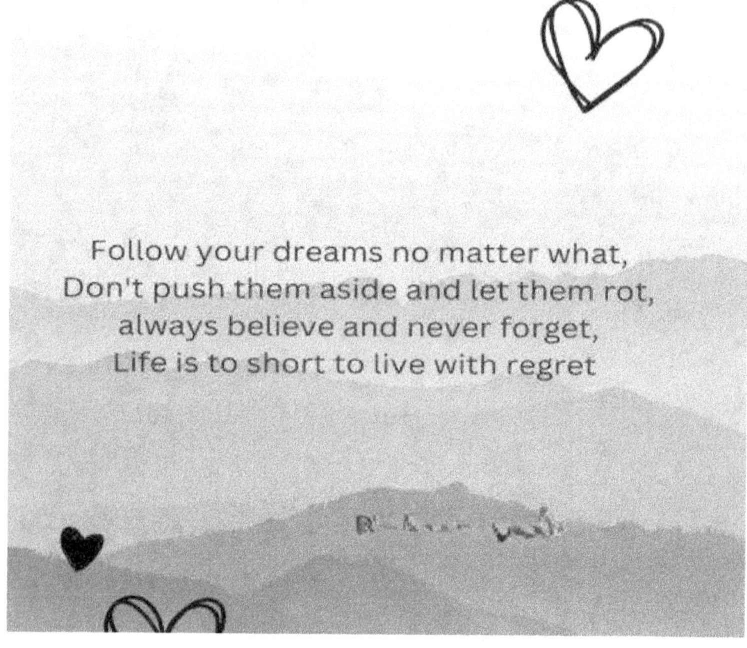

Seeing Life Through Different Lenses
Ashling McGee

Sometimes just sitting and silence
Clears the mind
never be afraid to be alone
As you can be in crowed room and still fell alone
the journey starts and ends with you

Live, Love, Dance
life brings highs and lows
But music can sooth the soul
Take a chance
And just Dance

Start over again
Blank canvas

Walk your own path
Find yourself
Change can be good

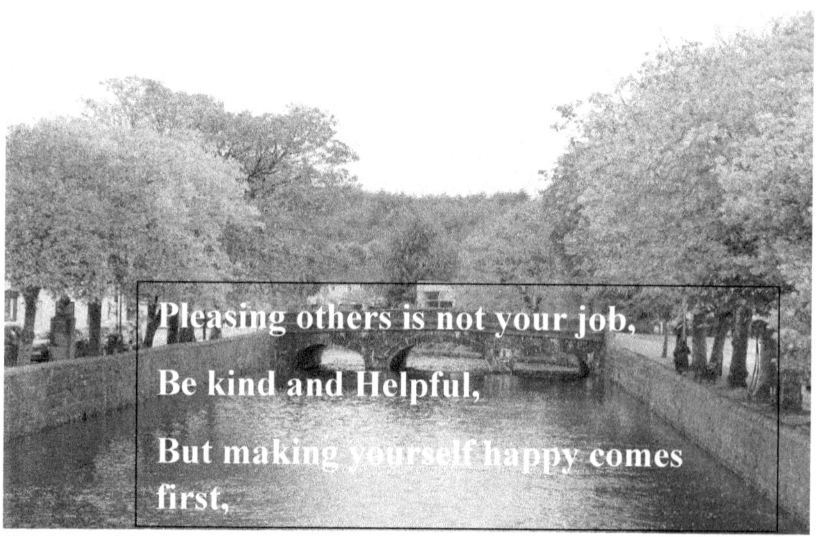

These created positive social media posts to give others a

positive outlook and improve society.

The other side shows how some struggle inside and hope for life to improve, not knowing what tomorrow may bring.

The following are self–perception views. You can agree or disagree with what is written. It gives an outlook on how one might see or judge themselves from one perspective. These stories show the different negative and positive outlooks on life.

Feeling weak and fearing the unknown

By Ashling McGee

Sasha wonders if her life would be different if she had opened that door instead of running away. Now, she is a working single mother, barely making enough to keep the vultures away from her door. Sasha wonders about another life she could have had if she had taken the risk. Wondering what could have been behind that door, she has all these ideas floating around. One night, Sasha gets home and pays the woman who looks after her daughter with the bit of money she has left. She only lives two doors down, is very kind, and knows that Sasha is hard-working and a single mum doing her best. She tells Sasha that Daisy is fast asleep and is a joy to mind. Sasha thanks the woman as she leaves. Sasha sits at the table after working a double shift at the Diner; exhausted and isolated, her head slowly drops to the table, her eyelids close, and she begins to drift away.

Drifting away, she begins to walk towards the door, feeling butterflies in her stomach, anticipating what lay beyond her. She reaches for the doorknob and starts to turn it every so slowly. You can hear it creak with each turn. She opens it ever so slightly, gasping for air with pure excitement. it opens a little, and she hears a voice calling, "Come on, you can do it; just one more push, and you are in." Sasha listened to the voice; she did not know why, but it gave her a shiver, and she opened the door. There was very little light in there, and she was nervous about stepping inside, but the voice called to her again, "Come on in; it is not that scary once you step inside." Sasha did not feel at ease and was scared, but she still felt drawn in by the voice, making her more interested in seeing what was inside. Still uncertain, Sasha walked in nervously into the unknown. Suddenly, the door slammed shut behind her, and now she was trapped. The voice shrieked with laughter, "Welcome to my funhouse." Sasha shivers with fear. What had she got herself into? She shouted, "Help! Help! Someone! Help me, please," all she could hear was her echo; nobody was going to save her now.

She began to walk toward the voice that was laughing at her. She wanted to see what was happening and how she could get out. As she began to walk, she could feel something at her feet trying to stop her from reaching the voice. She could only see what looked like vines wrapping around her feet with very little light. What the hell, she screamed? The voice shrieked again, "Try and catch me if you can." As the vines wrapped around her, Sasha fell to her feet and tried pulling away.

She shrieked, putting her hands in front of her, hoping there was something to grab. Suddenly, she felt something and held it. It was a cold metal of some sort and was strong enough that the vines released their grip." Good girl, the voice shrieked. You are trickier than you think". Sasha cried out, "What do you want from me." The voice laughed in a high pitch, saying, "Not me, dear; what is it you want? You entered my realm". Sasha cried and realised she did not know what to do but would not let this voice win. Standing up, learning a railing and stairway in front of her, she started to make her way upwards, wondering what else was in store. She walked up step by step in complete darkness, still hearing that voice, "Come on, girl, I have not got all day." Laughing with that high-pitched sound nearly drove Sasha to madness. As she climbed, she became more robust and wanted to fight this voice. She shouted, "I am coming for you, you wretched voice." Sasha found herself at the top of what seemed like a lifetime climb, but she felt a cold-shaped door handle. The voice shrieked, "You made it, my dear, how exciting! Let us see what awaits you behind this door," laughing as the voice faded.

Sasha did not know whether to open this door or return the way she came. She knew what awaited her back the way she came, but what awaited her ahead made her nervous. I do not think I can do this, but I must continue. I will not let this voice win; I cannot let it win. She opened the door gently, and as she did, she saw the light ahead of her. She pushed open the door further with excitement. As she stepped, she fell into what seemed like a hole. She screamed and thought, oh my god, this is it. I am going to die. Life flashed before her eyes, her daughter alone with nobody crying out for her mother. "Why, mum? why did you leave me?" Sasha's heart started to break. I cannot die now. My daughter would be left alone in this world. The voice came again, laughing. Look at you now, dying with nothing to show for your life and leaving a poor child alone without nobody; you are a disgrace.

Sasha shouted. I would not die and leave my daughter alone. You will not win. As Sasha began to fall deeper and deeper, she reached out and found something to grip. It was a ledge, but I clung to it for dear life. As she grabbed the edge, she pulled herself up and found it was an opening into another room. She did not care where it was if she was safe. The voice returned. I have to give you credit. You are a fighter. It makes it more attractive to see if you can get out. Let us know how you handle what is next, laughing as the voice fades.

Sasha wonders what could be next. She could not handle much more of this but was determined to get out to her daughter, which drove her to continue. As Sasha stood, hearing a moan or a growl of some sort. Oh no, what is it now, she thought. Still in complete darkness, trying to feel her way around, she felt a cold stone wall and tried to follow it around the room. Then, the growl came nearer and nearer. She saw these yellow eyes and felt them glaring at her. She was scared to move, did not know what to do, and heard the voice; this time, it was a whisper in her ear. The spokesperson said, "It is a wolf, so be very still, and he may go asleep, or you could try running for the next door if you can find it." The voice faded again.

Sasha was terrified. What could she do but be still and try to act invisible? Something Sasha was good at, feeling hidden most of her life. She had to get out to her daughter, so she had to do something. Sasha was moving silently towards the wolf. It was quiet and did not seem to hear her progress as she got nearer; however, it growled and became alert. Sasha stood still and could now see the wolf but did not move or show fear even though her heart was pounding. She stood tall and kept staring at the wolf, not moving an inch. The wolf then seemed to growl less. Its teeth seemed to relax, and then, out of nowhere, it lay down and closed its eyes. The voice returned, "Well done, you have put the wolf asleep, and now you may pass." As the voice disappeared, a door clicked open, and a light shone through. Sasha strolled towards the door and passed the wolf, silently in case he awoke again, but it did not, and she was safely in the next room.

This room was different. It was bright and vaguely saw certain things, and in front was a free-standing full-length mirror. She walked up to the mirror and looked at herself. Then the voice came from the mirror, but the person speaking was Sasha through the mirror. What is going on? Sasha asked. Sasha's image replied you made it, my dear. I have been the voice taunting you and making you feel everything. I was you the whole time. I have been the voice inside your head trying to get you to see yourself.

All those tasks were to show you that you are a solid and abled person. You doubted yourself and felt alone and isolated, but in reality, you are strong, can fight for what you want, and have a beautiful daughter who depends on and needs you. No matter how hard life gets, you can and will survive. It was a test, and you passed. You must realise you are not weak and can fight and keep the wolves away from the door. There is always help there. It would help if you asked; someone will help and guide you on the right path.

Now, you must decide what you want in life for yourself and your daughter. You must walk through this mirror, realise your potential, and fight for it. I do not know if I am strong enough to face the outside world, but I want to do my best for my daughter and show her that you can do anything your heart desires and have a great life if you fight for it and believe in yourself to do it. Sasha began to walk through the mirror. She could hear that voice saying, "Go on, you can do it. I believe in you". As she entered the mirror, she woke up and was dressed in her work uniform at her kitchen table. Her daughter stood there watching her sadly. ' are you all right, mummy? You look so tired,' she told her daughter that everything would be all right and started realising that she could do better and get there, and her daughter would have a better life because now she was not afraid to reach out and ask for help.

A week later, Sasha walks home from work but not from the diner where she worked. She called home and asked for help instead of trying to do things alone. It took much strength to make that call that she was dreading for so long. Her parents had argued with Sasha when they found out she was pregnant, and they fought about her throwing away her life and what she could accomplish if she had not gotten pregnant. Sasha felt alone and had done what she at that time was for the best and left to have the baby instead of staying there in judgement from her parents and fearing that they would not accept the baby that was now going to be part of her life. When she dialled that number, she did not know what to expect, but her parents were happy to hear from her, as she had walked away and they had never heard from her. They told her they were sorry for their reaction and never meant to make her feel alone and isolated. They worried about her and tried to find her but had no success. However, they never stopped loving her and hoped that she would come home when the time was right for her to do so. They were over the moon, and she was all right, and they finally met their granddaughter Daisy, whom they love and cherish so much. Now, she lives near them in a rented house. They help with babysitting while Sasha returns to finish her education and has a job as a receptionist at the local doctor, which she loves and is working on getting her degree in health care. She feels that life has taken a turn for the better. It was not easy ringing her parents and asking for help, but it was good for her and her daughter. Now, her daughter is happy, loves where she lives, and has made friends, and they both feel safe. Sometimes, we do what we think is correct, and we fear that going back or asking for help is a sign of weakness and that we cannot do things on our own. No matter how we try to do things on our own and want to feel like that to succeed, that is what you have to do, but reaching out when you need a helping hand shows more power and strength than you could imagine. It shows how strong you are as an individual and human being.

<u>**Which Direction**</u>

Have you ever felt alone in a crowded room, like you are unseen by anyone, just left isolated and tossed aside? You could be talking to someone, but are they listening to you?

A quiet, shy person, maybe not as career-driven as others, has a child or children to care for while dealing with their life struggles. Single parents and life throws so many curve balls, but we still have the strength to get up every day and fight to survive. Some say you have it easy as their careers are killing them working all hours, but what do they think a mother is? That job never stops. Some have a child, career, husband, great money, house, etc. Our lives take many journeys and paths but do not discard the ones you do not see. Every life tells a different story. So many hide away and cannot find the strength to do what others may do. Do not judge someone's life; every life is different and has problems. We all strive to survive in this world. Some do it better than others. It does not make them better than you.

Nobody should be made feel small or invisible or that their

life is inconsequential. We all are the same; we take

different journeys to get where we need to go and find

balance.

Asking For Help

There is no shame in asking for help. We all need it sometimes; it does not make you weak. It makes you strong, knowing that you cannot do it alone and asking for help is suitable. Everyone feels like they can handle everything independently, which is something to be admired, but it shows a strong survivor who can ask for help. It is not something you should be ashamed of but proud of; you are a strong individual who knows when you need a helping hand. There is always someone willing to help if you reach out and ask. Never be afraid to reach out when you need it. It has no shame; it is a sign of strength, not weakness. Believe in yourself and the people who love and care for you and are there for you when you need it most.

You've been hurt and
broken
Asking for help doesn't
Make you weak
It makes you a strong
Survivor

Walk The Path

The path we walk sometimes needs to be revised. It has twists and turns. It might lead us astray sometimes, but we get back on and keep walking. It will lead each of us to where we need to be. Trust in yourself and the mistakes you make. It all has a purpose and will lead us in the right direction no matter how far we may stray from the path. It is never easy and always a challenge, but keep walking on your path. You will get through it.

The road your walking
May not be easy or perfect
It will have obstacles
To overcome
but will lead you
To where you need to be

<u>Just Breathe</u>

Just forget the past. Forgive and forget. Just breathe and

forget those big Egos. For everything you love and make you

smile, laugh as much as possible and live life to the fullest.

Move forward and enjoy life on your terms and how you want

to.

<u>Find the Strength</u>

Believe in yourself. You are more powerful than you think. You can face any challenges you face. It would be best if you found the strength from within. There is no shame in asking for help if you need someone to lean on. Remember, you are never alone. Everyone has their weakness and strengths. Finding the strength to ask for help is more powerful and braver than facing problems alone. It is not a sign of weakness. It is a sign of great courage. Most of us struggle to deal with everything independently, but sometimes, help is needed, and the bravest thing is knowing when to ask for it.

Everyday Life is
A challenge
It is how we face
The challenge
determines our strength
But always remember
YOU ARE NEVER ALONE

Keep The Faith

Have faith in yourself; you may not know what is before

you, but believe in yourself and take a chance. This is your

journey; you can go anywhere and do anything if you open

your mind and move forward instead of staying still.

The Expectations BARBIE Has From Childhood To Adulthood

By Ashling McGee

When a child receives its first Barbie Doll, you can see the delight and sparkle in their eyes. At this age, their imagination flows out of them, and they believe they are in a magical place surrounded by all these beautiful things. A child reaches an age where reality hits them; they now have real friends and are too old to play with dolls. However, Barbie believes you must be slim and perfect to achieve greatness.

It takes away a teenager's self-confidence as if this is what I have to look like; I must be doing things wrong. I look ugly and fat, and I need to be slim and perfect. Barbie may give children, especially females, great power to believe they can do anything and be anything. There is a cost, as the concept of Barbie is to look good and be slim, and everything will fall into place.

This is unrealistic, as everyone is beautiful no matter what; they are unique. Yes, playing with dolls gives a child a sense of imaginative play, but to what extent does it become realistic to believe that is what you should look like to have these things in life? There are so many newer methods of influencing how one should look and achieve greatness by looking a certain way. This is nothing new. It has been going on for so long, and it will never evaporate from life.

The idea of feminism behind Barbie gives us women the belief that we can do and be anything if we put our minds to it. This is great in a world where women fight to survive in a man's world. However, it has given far more than expected, and now it seems women are becoming more potent in their own right. Where is the balance, and will there ever be an ideal world where all genders and sexes are equal and balanced?

Barbie is one of many societal tools influencing people to believe in a certain way. Even in adulthood, we all become susceptible to one's power of persuasion. Do we have minds of our own? Are we just robotic tools used to do one's bidding? Walt Whitman put it best.

"I exist as I am; that is enough." We should be who we are, not someone else's picture-perfect version. Now, we see how diverse we have become. Some are turning against trends and what is expected of them and living their way, which is how it should always be. To have a perfect life, be unique and not so perfect; that makes life interesting. If everyone were perfect, what kind of messed-up world would it be? BORING, that is what.

<u>Men's Idealistic Views on Women</u>
<u>Let's Dish It Out and Serve It Up For Public Opinion.</u>
<u>By Ashling McGee</u>

Okay, women, let us dish it and serve it up. Have men changed their romantic view of women from the past? Answer yes and no. Women today, of course, have changed. They are now more assertive, have more power, earn more money, and are self-sufficient, unlike when their job was to bear children and tend to household duties. Men have changed slightly but have not shifted much regarding how they see women. They have become more taciturn in how they pursue it. They still want women to be perfect and suit their needs. Women have now become more selective in the company they keep. This puts men at a disadvantage and makes them eager to change to gain some control over women. Women can now earn more than men, making some men feel isolated and less superior. However, some take advantage of the situation, letting women take control while they have fun and less stress as they are not the breadwinners and can have more fun. It makes the

women feel in control, having the power, but do they, when

men manipulate it to their advantage, they can cut loose

and have fun? In contrast, the women support the male

partner, leading to secret affairs and distance within

marriages. So that is much like the past, where men did

what they wanted but now have the option of not working

as hard as the women in the relationship, bringing in more

money. Women have to work twice as hard to gain respect

in the workforce. Even with women's rights, it is still a

man's world.

Women still have to compromise when it comes to

marriage and children. Fair enough, you have the new-age

man who will be a stay-at-home dad while the mother

works, but at what cost? A working mother misses out on

the child growing up and the bounds more with the father

than with you, which can be, in some cases, heartbreaking

for the mother. Women can choose this life, but the cost is

too high. Men still have power over certain situations.

Women strive to please men, whether it is through work or

home life. Their age, their beauty and the position they hold

in work. They may have gotten the same rights as men in

some aspects, but at a deadly price. Some may disagree

with my statement, and you have every right to. I am just

dishing and serving what I believe is happening. Men still

want women of stature in an excellent position to provide

for their beauty, bear children, and keep a happy household.

Some men comply and appreciate the women in their lives

by supporting and meeting them halfway, while others take

advantage and still want it all and have the power to control

the situation. So, the answer is yes and no; men have and

have not changed their ideological views on women.

A man is a male who makes a name for themselves

but still has time to fool around and play with women. At

the same time, women work hard to earn a name for

themselves and barely have time to meet a decent man.

Some women thrive on this and are happy just pushing and pushing for a career and making it in a man's world, but they lose something along the way. That can be a partnership or relationship as their time is taken up with work the whole time. Some women achieve it, which is excellent, and I bow down my head to those who can complete it all, but was it at the cost of something in your life? Do you feel that you missed out on something? Men fly by the seed of their pants and still come out on top. Do men feel like women do about losing something along the way, or do they have it easy? That is the question to answer.

Men have certain stages in their lives. The young male is a college party guy and many women along the way, although you cannot paint all men with the same brush. Then you have the career-driven man who does anything to climb the corporate ladder and still has time to get women. Still, now, maybe they are thinking more of women who will look good on your arm at an office party while hiding away women that the bosses would look down upon this

woman. She is not introduced to your business clients or

friends but is only seen at a motel or in the apartment, not

seen out in public. In a darkened restaurant, sit at the back

so nobody will notice you. Now, we move on to the man

looking for someone of great stature to bring home to his

mother. Women with class, good family breeding of high-

class society and highly educated. This looks good for the

company, a family man with women of prestige. This is the

woman you want to bear your children and start a family

life with. For some men, that is enough, but others still

have the mistress hidden away for the fun times and for the

man to escape the life they chose for themselves. We, as

women, are doing the same as men did back in older times

by being more decisive about whom we settle down with.

Is it for your position and what looks suitable for the

company, or is it for love? Have the tables turned? Now,

women have taken over the male role regarding prestige

and power. Of course, this is just one woman's opinion, but

does some of it ring true, or is it all a false misgiving of the

situation? I am just dishing it out and serving it up for

public opinion.

<u>Future self – By Ashling Mcgee</u>

Lilly always wondered what her future would hold. She was a senior in high school, and questions had been asked about where she saw herself in five years. Everyone asked this question. For Lilly, it was the most challenging question of what she would be doing in five years when she did not even know what she would be studying in college. Life seems to happen on a day-to-day basis for her. An assignment that had to be finished in a week was to write to her future self, which would be locked in a chest and opened again for the school reunion. Everyone was so excited about this and could not wait to start, but Lilly could not decide what to write as she sat at her desk and tried to write; her mind was blank. What would the future hold? What would I be doing? She thought about many ideas and things that could happen in the future. She would be married, have a great life and a lovely house, or maybe be alone, single, and impoverished. She asked her friends, and they all had their lives planned out to the exact date of their wedding. She could never think that far ahead. She went to the teacher and asked for guidance in completing her assignment. She looked at Lilly and told her to speak from her heart and not do what she felt others would want her to do but what she envisioned herself becoming. She went home and took out a pen and paper; this is what she wrote.

Dear Lilly,

It feels weird writing to my future self, but here it goes. Everyone expects great things from me to do well in school and attend university to become essential, but that is not me. Yes, I want to do and achieve something in my own time and my way. I am still determining where I will be in the future, but whoever I become will be my achievement rather than please others. I am trying to figure out what I want to become; I want to try many different things. That is what your youth is for. I want to travel, explore, learn all other beautiful things and then settle for something that will bring me happiness every day. As for love and marriage, well, that is a different story. Everyone desires to love and feel joy, and that includes me as well. I will not marry for being married at a certain age or the clock ticking on my life cycle. It is meant to be if love finds me, but I will not look for it. My future wish is happiness and joy in whatever I do. The future can hold so much and open many doors and paths. Does anyone know what will happen to them? Goodbye for now, and we shall see what the future holds.

Ten years had passed, and it was that time for the school reunion. Everyone was there, friends and classmates you had not seen since leaving for university. Some had great jobs; some were married, some divorced, and others were unrecognisable. As for Lilly, she was older but still the same in many ways. She had a job she loved, which took her worldwide. She had a great social life and good friends and had recently found the man she wished to spend the rest of her life with. One of her classmates asked her, 'How did you do it'?. She replied do what. Her classmate smiled, saying you look fabulous, not stressed, perfect, happy and contented with life. Lilly smiled. I followed my dream from the heart, not someone else's expectation of what I should become. Her classmate smiled. I wished I had done that and not followed the social form of what was expected of me. Lilly realised that most of her classmates had regrets and were unhappy in their skin and life. Lilly, however, had no regrets and was just purely happy with everything. They then opened the chest with their future letters inside. They all had to read them out in front of everyone as they read the papers of their great aspirations. Some people's sadness, bitterness and anger were falling apart at the seams. It came to Lilly, and as she read hers, everyone clung to her words and smiled and cheered when she finished. They told her that she was the one who had achieved greatness without any expectations and hoped that their children would follow in her footsteps in becoming a person who had no regrets and lived life the way they wanted, not following any social form or pressure from others to do as they expect them to do.

Life can turn out differently than you expect. The idea is to accept change as it may be your best possible future. Life is for living and doing it your way on your terms. Society shows us different possibilities. It is up to you to choose the path you want to take. The one question everyone wants to ask and wants an answer to is what the future holds for us. That is impossible, as people are still determining the future. You can choose one path and journey and then change, leading you to a different way entirely, but that is what life is for. It is living in the now and taking each day with new eyes, seeing where it leads and your journey. That is the most incredible adventure of all. Live life without regrets, as that keeps you from completing your journey.

<u>How mental health can be associated with where you see yourself in five years</u>

<u>By Ashling McGee</u>

That question haunted me as I did not know where I saw

myself five years from when I was twenty. One of those

questions is supposed to inspire you and make you think

about the future, but does it do that? Does it just add

pressure to where you are expected to be in five years, and

what exactly happens if you do not reach that goal you set

for yourself? Nobody can see their future, and whoever says they can is just pretending or being naive and maybe hoping that is where they will be. Life happens along the way. Yes, you may set dreams and goals and wish to achieve them, but there is no time limit on these goals and dreams. They can happen at any time in your life. So, do not expect to be where you believe you should be in five years. Anything can change in an instant. The path you wish to take can branch off to another direction entirely, so live life and do not follow someone else's expectations. It is your life, and you decide what happens in it. Life is for living, not trying to fixate on something that you may have said when you were eighteen and, in five years, be unhappy and disappointed that you did not achieve that goal. Look at your life and achievements, and remember that dreams are possible anytime. Everyone is different; some strive to get their position in life but miss out on the little things. Take each day as it comes. There is a way to work hard and live life. It is a balance, and finding that balance will bring clarity, less stress, and a better version of you.

Do not conform to your expectations to achieve and be the best. Just be who you are as time goes by quickly, and anything can happen. This kind of query that is asked of a young person can linger and haunt them, which in turn affects their mental health. They begin to panic if, in five years, they have not done what they have set out to do. Everything gets confusing and can upset people, especially if you are going to a school reunion where you have set goals and your friends you have not seen in so long have accomplished their goals. Still, you might not have as you have taken a different path or road to get there, which might take longer, but at that particular time, you do not see it. All you see is how everyone else's life seems to be bigger, better, and more prosperous. However, they are also struggling to keep up with the busy lifestyle they have created, and at the end of it all, they are lonely and tired and feel life is not worth it. There are always two sides to a

coin, as they say. It can flip either way, but the result is the

same: everyone struggles, no matter their chosen path. The

best route is finding a balance, which is quite tricky, but it

is worth it when you do. Life is so much better, and you

feel happier within yourself, the stress is less, and you can

enjoy all the little things in life and continue to reach your

goal with a much better frame of mind and clarity.

When you are in your twenties, you feel like you can

conquer the world, and that is a great attitude, but do not let

it become an obsession, as you may miss out on all life has

to offer. While you are busy conquering the world, life is

passing you by; you are too focused and do not take the

time to enjoy the moments that will disappear if you allow

them. Mental health is a big concern for all people. Still,

sometimes it is drilled into you when you finish school that

you must have this or must do this to succeed, which can

cause anxiety and mental health problems when you get to

your thirties and feel like you have missed out on the best parts of living life enjoying the little things each day. There is a fine line between being over-focused and needing more focus. We all need a small quantity of both, where we can focus on what we want out of life and live in the moment. That is where the balance comes in. You will flourish once you find your balance, and the weight on your shoulders will lift once you find it. You can breathe much easier, control life, and live the life you want and deserve.

Sometimes, pressure comes from the parents in wanting their child to do well and have a better life than they had. In reality, look at your parent's life and see how they struggled and worked hard, but are they happy? Do they seem content and still have time for the little things in life? If they do, you can see that they found a balance that works for them and tell them you would be happy if your life turned out as content and comfortable as theirs. Parents want the best for their children and maybe put too much pressure on them to achieve a better life. Remember that it is up to you how you want to live your life, but dreams are always attainable no matter how you travel to get them.

Life is complicated and complex. Once you reach adulthood, the choices are yours, and you must deal with the consequences of your actions. It is called living and finding your way to a better version of yourself, finding that inner strength and balance that gives you peace of mind, and obtaining your goals. Mental health is a struggle, but remember that there is always someone to help, and you are never alone as others struggle with issues as well. Always feel in the right place. Life can change in an instance, and when you think that you are in a dark place, remember there is a light, and it shines for you, and it will guide and help you in finding your way back on the path to finding the person you are and were always but just needed a little help in finding yourself. Once you do, life will open and flourish, and all those little moments will appear.

Sylvia Plath's "The Bell Jar" concerns a young woman's struggle for self-determination.

By Ashling McGee

Plath's novel is a well-documented account through

style and narrative of written words and imagery. This is

shown by Plath absorbing herself into the novel through the

character of Esther Greenwood, who is written in the style

of flashbacks of different events during Esther's life.

Esther is trying to find her identity and a sense of belonging

in a society that she feels is restricting her and keeping her

prisoner to domestic duties, not allowing her to be herself.

Esther begins to lose herself and fall downwards into a

depressive state of negative thoughts that surround her past

and current choices. The reader gets to follow Esther's

story of descent into and out of a mental breakdown. This

shows the readers a sense of madness and sanity within

Esther. She immersed herself in this novel by seeing how

Plath uses the style and narrative of her words and imagery,

showcasing these through Esther, a talented young girl with

aspiring ambitions. These choices are in front of Esther, but

she has a feeling of negativity in which she struggles to

gain control of her life, make choices, and even the choices

that society presents to her.

From the very beginning till the very end, Plath exposes

the reader to the struggles of Esther Greenwood, her mental

downfall into an isolated negative person in her life choices

and what society has to offer. Esther, a young lady, gets a

scholarship to college, winning prizes, which leads her to

New York for a summer job in a fashion magazine, all

expenses paid. Instead of feeling happy and excited about

this opportunity, she feels motionless and still. 'I was not

steering anything, not even myself. I just bumped from my

hotel to work, and to parties, and from parties to my hotel. I went back to work like a numb trolley bus. '(Bell Jar 2). Feeling like she is not in control of her life and the way it is going, she feels isolated in a state of paralysis, as if life is moving and she is just pushed along. 'The silence depressed me. It was not the silence of silence. It was my silence'. (Bell Jar 17). From the very beginning, Plath was cleverly deep and intentionally intense in the way she narrated her writing as she understood the effect it would have on her readers. The reader can almost feel Esther's silence by the way it is written. You are immersed in Esther's mind of thought and feeling. Plath's novel moves people in a way we are influenced to feel with or through Esther Greenwood. The bell jar offers insights both towards mental health and selfhood. It describes how a person who has so much in her life but still feels isolated and alone falls into a depressive state as making decisions or choices seems impossible or out of reach.

Esther becomes haunted by images of marriage and motherhood. This is seen through the image of Buddy Willard's mother weaving this beautiful rug. She spent her time doing it, only to have its beauty spoiled in days by using it as a kitchen mat. Esther sees this negatively because a man only wants a wife laid out like a kitchen mat despite all the love and flowers. When Esther returns home, Plath shows a life that Esther could have. This is demonstrated through her neighbour Dodo Conway, who went to Barnard and married an architect—now living in a big house and pregnant with her seventh child. 'I could not see the point of getting up. I had nothing to look forward to. (Bell Jar 113). Esther considers a life choice she could have through her neighbour, Dodo Conway. In a way, Esther is jealous of Dodo, and her neighbour has a life that is the life she wants. Esther rebels against this, seeing herself as other than a wife, but does not want to give up the female experience of loving someone, having children, and leading a satisfied domestic life. Conflicted by wanting it all,

Esther sees it through a negative lens.

The plot line of the fiction is in the journey itself, and

the journey is to find a symbol or a sign to approve the trip.

In Plath's novel, the fig tree is imagery that could be a

symbolic part of the novel. This is where Esther sees her

life branching out before her like the green fig tree. Each

figure represents a specific academic choice, such as

poetry, publishing, marriage and children. There are so

many figs that it is hard to see beyond the tree, and making

choices she wants is complex with so much on offer. 'I

saw myself sitting in the crotch of this fig tree, starving to

death just because I could not decide which figs I would

choose. I wanted every one of them, but choosing one

meant losing all the rest, and as I sat there, unable to

decide, the figs began to wrinkle and go black and one by

one, they plopped to the ground at my feet.'(Bell Jar 73).

Plath is conveying here that as soon as a woman leaves her

family unit to live alone and start life by herself in society,

they are fallen from grace, not complying with what society

expects of them. This is Esther, who wants to live outside

society's norm. She is seen as a failure or has fallen from

grace as she rebels against what she should comply with

within the society she lives in—wanting to choose a

different life than the life seen by society but still wanting

some part of the society's norms, such as being a wife and a

mother. Esther wants a domestic life but much more: to be

able to do things outside the natural order. The fig tree

represents choices that Esther has to make, and those fallen

leaves could represent her fall from grace or a failure to

choose as she wants it all. 'Esther is told repeatedly that her

choices, while hers to make, will have repercussions she

cannot control'.(Janet Badia 133). The sense of not having

control over choices is seen in Esther's rebellious attitude,

which is clearly shown through Plath's narrative in Esther's reaction to the Negro kitchen worker in the Psychiatric ward in the hospital.

The negro kitchen worker shows Esther's rebellious or spoiled child-like attitude. The kitchen worker comes to serve the food at her table in the hospital; Esther is unhappy about his insufficient presentation of the choice of food he serves her. I was disgusted that it was beans and beans, which should never happen as this is no choice. It should be beans and carrots or beans and peas. The lack of choice she faces means she behaves like a spoilt child who already has too many choices and should be happy to have none at all. The negro kitchen worker calls her Miss Mucky Muck; on hearing this, Esther kicks him on the calf of the leg. 'That is what you get, I said and stared him in the eye'.((Bell Jar 175). Esther is acting out as she has no control over anything, as there is no choice, but the kitchen worker sees her as a spoilt brat with choices that he wishes he had as he is limited due to the colour of his skin. 'Soon after they had locked the door, I could see the Negro's face, a molasses-coloured moon, rising at the window grating, but I pretended not to notice'.(Baldwin 35). Plath shows the readers an image which is of a black kitchen worker peering into a white woman's room of imprisonment but could also be looked at as the negro worker peering out of his imprisonment. Plath's writing style here gives the reader an image of a person of colour who goes unnoticed as others pretend not to notice that he even exists in the society that they live in. 'The book offers the enticement of national narratives that proffer integrated selfhood as a warning that we may, like Esther, pretend to notice'. (Baldwin 37). Plath has the freedom to choose what to tell her readers by using characters that seem to go unnoticed, like the negro giving him no name but still makes an impact on how she portrays him in the novel. She uses her writing style and imagery to make an impression on her audience while relating to racial and ethnic images shown throughout the book. Plath achieves this without overpowering or taking away from Esther's story and her struggle with overcoming her mental stability.

As the narrative composition shows, Esther Greenwood's story is built with fragments of past experiences seen through the lens of present events. The reader is constantly informed of the importance of these past experiences. Plath does this from the beginning, like the image of the cadaver Esther first saw; she links this to Buddy Willard as a balloon on a string that she carries with her and is everywhere in her mind. 'Plath forces several scenes, objects and reflections into the fragmented but relentless stream that makes up Esther's consciousness'. (Linda Wagner Martin 31). Another image is the Fig Tree, which symbolises life choices and Esther's journey connected to the tree. Plath uses characters that link Esther's consciousness. There is a link between Joan's death and Esther's rebirth; the unsuspected suicide is

Plath's imagined event in the novel. This is Plath's emotional understanding of the text. Joan, who falls in love with another woman, can pursue a career and a life of independence without a man or marriage. This character must die for the demons that haunt Plath's / Esther's mind to be purified. The rebirth of Esther is not a new strong self but a woman who gives into her fear of love and nurture of women.

At the novel's end, despite Doctor Nolan's reassurance, Esther was scared to death, hoping to feel sure about what lay outside the door. Esther could still see question marks. ' There ought, I thought, to be a ritual for been born twice patched, re-treaded and approved for the road'.(Bell Jar 233). Plath uses her writing style to leave readers wondering if Esther found her life's choice outside the hospital or if she spiralled again out of control. It was an exciting or intentional play by Plath to make us aware of whether anybody is sure of their choices, whether they comply with what society wants them to do, or if they rebel

and end up confused and isolated from everyone and

everything. Not making a particular choice and wanting

more and more can lead to inevitable confusion and

consequences that you must live in your life. Plath's style

and narrative use in the novel draw the reader in from the

beginning to the end. Plath's subdivisions of plots or

episodes refer to the past and present, leading the reader

through events of madness and sanity altogether. This

involves readers with Esther Greenwood, maybe seeing

parts of themselves in her life's journey and coping

struggles.

12 Years A Slave – Book vs Film and the lens we see it through.

By Ashling McGee

Readers are immersed in a world of strange and surreal events when reading a book. However, when reading a book like "12 Years a Slave", which is based on actual true events, it brings a whole new meaning. Unlike adventure, drama or mystery novels where your mind is opened to an array of possibilities, "12 Years a Slave" brings you up close and personal with one man's torture and pain, which he lived through daily. Solomon Northup's memoir accounts for a man's life as an enslaved person. Slavery is one of the significant human catastrophes in human history. In America, the legacy of slavery, born of native racism, is still relevant in today's society. Both history and memory speak about slavery and the experience of African people held in American captivity but spoken in different tongues. When both history and memory meet, the results can be unpleasant. The release of Steve McQueen's film 12 Years A Slave gives the audience an in-depth viewing of enslaved people and their treatment as objects, not actual human beings at all. It is not for the faint-hearted, with such graphic and gory subjections of enslaved people and how they were treated. Questions are asked: Does the film represent Solomon Northup's memoir? Some strengths and weaknesses are shown throughout, but it is still a profound masterpiece of work that Steve McQueen displays in his production 12 Years a Slave.

As someone who always prefers reading and finds a book so much more accurate and detailed than a film, I was taken in by Steve McQueen's production. There have been other films that have displayed American slavery but in a reversed role. Take, for instance, 'Gone With The Wind', a classic movie everyone has watched at some stage in their lifetime. It represents a privileged white woman and her affair with a man in the American South during the Civil War. The representation of slavery is merely a backdrop, and slavery is seen through rose-tinted spectacles and even romanticising the treatment of black people in the South. They were seen as happy and enjoyed their positions within their master's house. They were treated as ordinary employees and rewarded with gifts for loyal service. This representation is subjective to the audience, showing that slavery was not as horrific as it is made out to be, giving pause to how history was represented in the film industry. McQueen's production gives you an up-close personal account and a raw experience that leaves its audience sick to their stomachs. Leaving an ever-lasting imprint on what life was actually like for an enslaved person. 12 Years a Slave breaks down the narrative between the actual slavery event and the film's representation, which invites all to think about the relationship between the exact text and the film's portrayal.

McQueen captures a film that humanised a glazed-over historical act of brutality through a person's eyes, showing necessary restraint. This is shown in the movie when Solomon, now an enslaved person named Platt, sings with fellow plantation enslaved people, overcome with hopelessness, his voice getting louder and growing in strength, singing about souls rising from the earth. The pain is shown clearly due to the close-up on his face, but it gives an inspired feeling as he is now broken into the reality of the life stolen from him. It allows him to be rescued by this promise of kingdom come. It shows that light seeps out even when in the darkest place you could be in. The film presents violence, which is the critical motive for showing 12 Years A Slave as an accurate portrayal of slavery. McQueen uses darkness and shadows in certain scenes, showing Northup's life now with ruthless beatings where he declares he is a freeman. The dark, damp room gives the viewers a feeling of loneliness that Northup now feels isolated, alone and now an enslaved person captive. The journey ahead will be brutal and complex, and the viewers feel this resonates with him as he knows what it will be like. McQueen uses images of pure violence to capture exactly what was done to Solomon. The novel is quite different as it uses vivid details in words of the brutality he suffered with the first beating: "He disappeared and in a few moments returned with these instruments of torture. The paddle, as it is termed, in an enslaved person beating parlance…. Was a piece of hardwood eighteen or twenty inches long, moulded to the shape of an old fashioned pudding stick or ordinary oar" (Northup, 41). This is what Northup saw and felt; his description is vivid, and the reader can imagine what it was like for him. McQueen shows us through images and sound, and darkened shadows enhance Northup's writing. He uses the pieces of written words and accurately replaces them with such embodiments, sounds, and darkened shadows to make the viewer feel what Solomon thought at that exact moment.

McQueen's focus on images shows the actual torture of an enslaved person. The scene that displays it creatively is when Solomon hangs from the tree with a noose around his neck; his arms and legs are bound, and his feet barely tip the ground beneath him. The camera lingers on this for a long time, captivating the audience and giving them a feeling of his suffering and what he endured. It was only minutes for us. For Solomon, it was days, but the audience gets that feeling as the camera lingers there, focused on him and only him. The book describes Solomon's pain and suffering: "My wrists and ankles and the cords of my legs and arms began to swell, burying the rope that bound them into the swollen flesh". (Northup, 146). It describes what was being done and how the burning sun beat down on his head, but McQueen's production style brings it to life with just the camera lingering there on Solomon, helpless and in pain. Even within the background, enslaved people carried on with their chores, children playing, but it was as if the camera just froze time as you stopped and watched Solomon. Did not notice anything around him. His face, expressions, and actions transfixed you as everything else carried on. This is where memory and history collide in some ways. McQueen is trying to bring these two to intertwine together so that they complement each other using Northup's memoirs and the history of slavery to showcase that these are the facts and that this is history through its purest form by an accurate account of someone who lived through it. Of course, you will have criticism about specific facts that may be over the top and do not fit the history of slavery as historians would see it. Still, from someone who lived to tell his side of the story, McQueen gives the viewers a more subjective form to decide what happened to enslaved people, humanity, and our world.

In some parts, McQueen embellishes his telling of Solomon's life story. This can be seen through Robert's death as in the film it was elaborated to a stabbing of Robert upon the slave ship Solomon was travelling on. This violence was McQueen's fabrication, which has no part in Solomon's memoirs. McQueen does this to show how violent life was for enslaved people, even though over-dramatised. It does fit Northup's narrative in the text. In the novel, the actual death of Robert is he dies of smallpox. When Solomon writes about Roberts's death, he says, "The inanimate body of poor Robert was consigned to the white waters of the gulf". (Northup, 81). It described his lifeless body being thrown away like garbage to the sea by white men and disposed of like an object or animal with no use anymore. This is the way the enslaved people were treated like non-humans. McQueen gives viewers a film that subjects everyone to observe the ideas surrounding humanity. In this visual display of slavery, McQueen shows that slavery is not just about brutalisation and victimisation; slavery was the infliction of violence and death, but also it was about life. Those who were forced to be enslaved did not surrender to the brutal violence that was being inflicted upon them. The enslaved people refused to be dehumanised by this barbaric treatment by others who treated them like animals and possessions they claimed ownership of.

One cannot imagine the culture of America without even considering the legacy of slavery. The dehumanisation force of slavery and how the enslaved people refused to be dehumanised shows how memory and history differ. History and memory do not combine naturally, as they differ in many ways. This division continues in today's society, where American freedom is always questioned. This great land of liberty and the land of the free is always in question as to what freedom is and who gains it. They are rules which restrict those from being free. This refers to the dehumanisation of enslaved people and anybody of different coloured skin. They are seen as a minority, but they refuse to be dehumanised and fight for what they should already have: a life of their own free will. McQueen's production brings to light these educational, raw, vivid images that give an in-depth insight into events. He tries to combine history and memory, most naturally and brutally possible, to give the viewers a lasting impression of the degradation of humanity. It provides those who look at the film with a profound perspective of life as an enslaved person and the horrific violence they suffered in their lifetime. Some may criticise McQueen's work as historians may argue that it is not historically correct, and that is their job, of course, but when you have a source with first-hand knowledge of what has happened, is this a primary source that one can stand up in an academic world. That is the question I believe McQueen is asking: Are memory and history separate or a connection that both can work together? It is one of those questions that is as old as time and one that lingers within America, those that remember the past and those of historical facts. The enslaved people's memories are haunted by what has happened, and it is never forgotten that it is their right always to refuse to be dehumanised, even in today's world. McQueen's film displays the enslaved person's psychological process better than the book could ever possibly do. It uses images taken from the novel and shows them in raw, gripping ways that make the viewers react and think. It is about survival, which exceeds one's impermanence.

<u>Literature Lens</u>

This lens explores how life can be seen through the lens of literature. One can read great literature and see different aspects of life flourish through it. How influential some are by the words they write. Literature is a great way to see past and present lives unfolding and how they might change the future, even if the past has changed in the present if things are still similar, and what can be done to change it for future generations. We all learn from the past, but is it life-changing in the direction it should, or are some things still stuck in the past, unable to move forward? Life changes. That is something we know, but great literature teaches something new, opens our eyes to what we can learn from it, and helps change our present and future selves. There are so many great works of Literature out there. These are just some things that have given me insight into life from the past and present.

<u>Women's Roles in Shakespearean plays Macbeth and Othello</u>

<u>By Ashling McGee</u>

Shakespeare's plays 'Macbeth' and 'Othello' bring to light two women who both play a significant role as developed characters in their respective plays. Both plays are a mix of violence and tragedy, with both women having tragic consequences. Shakespeare implanted a state of consciousness in two characters by whispering. These characters manipulate the situation by whispering in Macbeth and Othello's ears, making them believe what they say is true. In 'Macbeth, Lady Macbeth manipulates her

husband into killing to gain power and prestige. In

'Othello,' Iago manipulates Othello into believing that his

wife Desdemona is unfaithful. These two women wanted a

sense of freedom and control, but they both displayed a

sense of guilt in different ways.

Lady Macbeth is a character of strength and willpower at

first glance. Then, you discover a sensitivity within her that

makes her the inferior sex to male rulers. Lady Macbeth is

assertive, unlike her husband, who is very uncertain of

things. You can see this in Act 1, where she says:

"….. Come you spirits

That tends on mortal thoughts, unsex me here,

And fill me from the crown to the toe top-full

Of direst cruelty."

It shows that Lady Macbeth is as fearless as a man is

supposed to be. She displays a masculine side in that she

can do the blood deeds to achieve the crown, telling her

husband to leave it to her to plan everything. Macbeth may

be ambitious but is filled with human kindness, unlike his

wife, who shows no traits. In 'Othello,' Desdemona defies

her father by marrying a black Christian Moor in secret,

which dismantles her father's masculinity and can be seen

as shameful to take his masculinity away, especially by his

daughter. Shakespeare chose Venice to set his scene as,

back then, it was a city of sexual tourism. Men's and

women's relationships are not confined by marital status.

Infidelity is inevitable, but Desdemona is not true as she is

a faithful wife. Iago's hands turn Othello into a jealous

beast. Iago's suggestive tales send Othello into a rage of

jealousy, believing that his wife is a whore. It then has a

tragic end for Desdemona. Her death inspires sorrow for

her not because she is a weak woman but because of her

courage to stand and speak out for Cassio, whom Othello

believes she is having an affair with and defying her

father's will by travelling with her husband, Venetian

Empire, in Cyprus. Both are strong women on two similar

paths, both having tragic consequences.

At the start of Macbeth, Shakespeare shares a quote, "Fair

is foul, and foul is fair" (Act 1.1); the reversed role is in

Macbeth. Lady Macbeth fits into disorder as having male

traits pouring evil into MacBeth's ears. She begs the spirits

to "unsex her." His wife henpecks Macbeth, constantly

questioning his authority, telling him he is weak and unable

to carry out his duties as a man. She controls the first part

of the play with her speeches on gender and that manhood

is categorised by how much blood they can bleed from

killing. The blood represents the journey of murders that

she has inflicted and soon becomes her symbol of guilt for

what she has done. In 'Othello,' Shakespeare uses a

symbolic item, a silk handkerchief. It is a gift that Othello

gives Desdemona, showing a bond between them. It

represents fidelity and loyalty in their marital union; losing

this gift shows infidelity and dishonesty. In Scene 3, Act 4

"……And bid me, when my fate would have me wived,

To give it to her: I did so, and take heed do not,

Make it a darling like your precious eye:

To lose or give away were such perdition."

Showing the importance of the handkerchief, she does misplace it. She is filled with guilt as she knows her faith is locked; though it was an accident, her husband believes her dishonest, especially at the hands of Iago's whispering. Iago places it upon Cassio's possessions, enraging Otello even further, and Desdemona's death is now inevitable.

Lady Macbeth presents a different side that is more humanised, showing her female traits of remorse and sensitivity—consumed by guilt, the blood that stains her hands filled with the horrific acts. She is in a state of madness, unable to sleep in a paranoid, disillusioned state. One cannot help feeling sympathy for her as a person or a victim of her undoing. A woman trying to be as powerful as a man becomes undone by her traits as a female. She must pay for her sins by death. In 'Othello,' we see Desdemona now as a victim of Iago's doing. She slowly surrenders to the faith which is now in front of her as she tells Emilia (Scene 4 Act 3),

…." She was in love, and he she loved proved mad

Moreover, they did forsake her. She had a song of 'Willow.'

And old this was, but it expressed her fortune,

And she died singing it: that song tonight,

Will not go from my mind: I have much to do."

Her guilt from losing her precious gift that her husband entrusted her with now knows she has lost her husband to rage and has forsaken him somehow. Both women display guilt. 'Macbeth, we see it through Lady MacBeth's acts of staging murder for power. 'Othello' is one of conflict with Desdemona, as seen through Othello's eyes as dishonesty and infidelity. He wants Desdemona to be obedient but feels she is unfaithful at the persuasion of Iago's whispering. It is reversed in 'MacBeth' as it demands obedience from her husband in carrying out acts of murder

as a man should do to gain control. In turn, chaos is evident

amongst them all.

Great Writers of American Literature, their influence and powerful words!

By Ashling Mcgee

American literature in the hands of two great men of their time signifies similarities and individuality within their work. Whitman's rejection of traditional form illustrates regrowth both in public and political form. Langston Hughes's simultaneous rejection of and working within Whitmanian and Emersonian literature demonstrates a diverse political and racial self-assertion. Both influential figures use language to convey strong messages to manifest that "Past and present and future are not disjoined but joined." Looking at how Emerson influenced Whitman and how Whitman then influenced Langston Hughes, there are similarities between their work and a different point of view expressed through their language. While some stood on the sidelines of humanity, evoking power and influence through their words, others immersed themselves in the mix of the people, addressing them personally and making a difference through speech and poetry. Regarding religion with both Whitman and Langston Hughes, Whitman was a religious pessimist who thought that the human soul was immortal and in the process of developing. Langston Hughes opposed religious institutions but believed in sin, redemption, and atonement. Hughes wanted to celebrate the African American religious culture as its own identity rather than society's institutions.

Whitman responded to Emerson's work as Whitman also rejected the traditional form of poetic rhythm. Whitman was a passionate and mystic man. Whitman makes his presence felt in what he writes for others to read.

He, like Emerson, shares a type of transcendentalism. This can be seen through Emerson's work in "Nature" when he says, "The production of a work of art throws a light upon the mystery of humanity. A work of art is an abstract or epitome of the world". The mystery of humans is like a piece of art; only when all pieces fit can you see perfection within humanity. It shines light upon the pieces that mystify humanity. Emerson wanted everyone to see a new beginning, a new God and a new body to become immersed in one's surroundings. He wanted everyone to be one with nature, appreciate it, and protect nature, as Emerson saw it as a link with God himself. His written word on "Nature" is compelling and influenced Whitman's writing.

Like Emerson, Whitman went through a phase of self-recognition in which both the world and self were made new. Whitman desired praise from one man, Emerson; he received it in a letter that Emerson sent him. Walt Whitman had it printed in a newspaper and put it in his first edition of "Leaves". Walt Whitman was an

individualist man. His work states that all are equal, as we

all have immortal souls. His poem "The Sleepers" is a work

of art questioning life, death, and the limitations of a human

being. He discussed native American life and how

everything returns to its rightful order after mourning a past

soul. All gathered to mourn but dispersed in different

directions after the mourning period. His description of

"The Asiatic and African are hand in hand; the European

and American are hand in hand". He bestows his readers

that order out of place is good and order in its place is

terrible. It is a diverse set with limitations, as everything

and everyone belongs in a particular order. Walt Whitman,

a great poet of democracy, never really connected himself

as a person who sought to abolish slavery. Whitman argued

against abolition, along with his personal feelings about the

faith of African Americans. This, however, never went any

further than his aspiration to Keep African Americans from

mixing with White people. Whitman tries to evoke regrowth and shine a light on the diversity surrounding everyone. Whitman uplifted Lincoln's political commitment, feeling a political pull between himself and Lincoln in preserving the union to an artistic ideal. The imagery used in Whitman's book is like poetry, rejecting conventional form by positioning the poet with working-class people. Whitman's influential work inspired Langston Hughes.

Langston Hughes, a poet of the people, is a significant influencer of the Harlem Renaissance. While the Harlem Renaissance was not fully contained in the Harlem district of New York City, it served as a symbolic capital of cultural awakening. The Harlem Renaissance was a phase of a prominent New Negro people movement in a time when artistic experimentation took place. It caused African American rational thinkers to look at their heritage with fresh looks and a deep desire to reconnect with a heritage that both people of colour and white people misunderstand.

Whitman influenced him and became a more political racial

self-assertion. A world traveller and a writer in most

genres. His work is derived from a life he knows, which is

of racial treatment of African Americans like himself. He

heard America calling like Whitman and protested his right

to sing America black. Choosing to focus his work on

modern black life, confronting a political point of view

demanding African Americans be recognised for the

culture they attributed to creating America. His poem "I

Too" is a bold statement to America stating he should be

treated equally. Like Whitman, "The messages of great

poets to each man and woman are, come to us on equal

terms, only then can you understand us". Langston Hughes

carries this message further, stating, "I too am America." he

hears my words, refusing to be sent away to hide from the

person he is and will not be seen as an outsider looking in.

Langston's poetry is steeped in violence and a failing of Christianity. The powerful poems with a religious element are the ones in which he used Christ as a central figure. In Langston's poems about religion, sometimes "Christ is white which symbolises the oppressors and acts as their accomplice and other times Christ is black the image and friend of the lynched Negro and the one who suffers with him". This can be seen in Langston's work on "Christ in Alabama", which states that Christ is of coloured skin and beaten into submission by his white master. In one way, it is trying to take Christianity away from those who are prejudiced towards anybody with coloured skin. It is given back to the white master, as in Alabama, as Christianity serves at the hands of a white person. It is a powerful piece of poetry which forces you to listen and take notice of the political structure at play within the South. Another poem that catches a reader's attention is "Dreams," a short poem that is so captivating that you cannot help feeling connected. It is about holding on to your dreams as the world is brutal enough. Keeping hold of something makes it more bearable, and the future of your dreams awaits you if you hold on tight to it. The loss of such dreams can leave you cold and have no joy where nothing will grow for you. Can we compare this to Emerson's "Nature"? Hughes wants us to hold faith and our dreams as our future. Emerson wants us to have faith in our belief that nature and God are connected. There is a similarity within the links in which we hold our link to our surroundings and believe that God is present in some form to help guide us. Langston forces those to open their eyes in a political form to see what is happening to Christianity.

Whitman and Langston both reject traditional forms, using a platform to state their political views and using their language in expressive forms to enhance their ideologies. Both evoke regrowth and shine a light on diversity, changing political minds and shaping America's outlook on humanity. "The art of art, the glory of

expression and the sunshine of the light of letters is

simplicity". It can be easy for any one person to write

something so simple and have a profound impact on those

around you. To make a difference in both Langston

Hughes's and Walt Whitman's rejection of traditional form

reaches the minds of many through the simplicity of words

that society endears in their works of art. Hughes targeted

his readers by changing one's opinion on race. He was

influenced by Walt Whitman, wanting to make a difference

regarding race. Walt Whitman's "I Hear America Singing"

helped shape Langston Hughes's poem "I Too Sing

America". Both similar and effective, Langston Hughes

built on Walt Whitman's poem and how it affected people

and society. In Walt Whitman's poem "I Hear America

Singing", freedom is a cause for celebration in America. In

contrast, Langston Hughes's poem "I too sing America"

shows how America views him as an African–American,

his colour and how he is treated differently. He sings that

one day, he will be treated as beautiful, and those who

treated African Americans differently will feel shame.

Both Langston Hughes and Walt Whitman have

similarities in their work as they are democratic. They

believe in the possibilities of realising the American Ideal.

They both want America to be new again or become reborn

in a way. They both write about matters that cause concern

in a political form. They strive to make a difference.

Hughes is more outspoken, speaking for the people and

what is happening around him. Walt Whitman was more

conservative, whereas Langston grabbed your attention and

was for the people. Although Whitman was against the

abolition of slavery, he never went much further than his

aspirations, as Langston Hughes drove it forward with

more force and a more political stance. Hughes wanted

unity among people socially, economically, and culturally,

not just with the people of America but worldwide. They

were both great poets of their time and dealt with the

present and the future within their writing. Hughes wrote

about religion in his work and focused more on its racial

feeling in his poetry. "He views religion in the larger

context of black culture, presenting it variously as a source

of strength for the oppressed, an opiate of the people, the

religion of slavery, and an obstacle to emancipation." It is

interesting to see how others influenced each poet,

Emerson, Whitman, and Langston Hughes, and how they

carried their work further in a more political outlook,

showing the reader what was happening within their

timeline and the words they used to convey their message.

Still to this day, readers are amazed and captivated by the

words of these great writers of their time and in the hope of

influencing the next generation of writers that come along

to write something profound and that captivates the

attention of other people to listen and take notice of what is

happening within our society today.

How are Gender and Sexuality explored in the literary work of

"Frankissstein: A Love Story" by Jeanette Winterson

By Ashling Mcgee

Frankissstein: A Love Story is a modern-day version of the novel Frankenstein by Mary Shelley. The industrial revolution in Frankenstein is replaced with a contemporary narrative that features artificial intelligence, cryogenics, and sexbots. The novel Frankissstein involves a transgender doctor named Ry, a modern-day version of Mary Shelley. The story is plotted by questions of whether a body can be without a soul and whether a soul can function without a body. Winterson implements gender and sexuality throughout the novel. Gender is something that defines a person, but Winterson allows the reader to explore gender

as non - non-constricted or undefining by Ry as they are

transgender. Neither described as a woman nor a man opens

the door to redefining what gender is. Winterson shows this

through Ry's story of self-observation and being judged by

others, especially the males whose dominance over the

females is perceived as the weaker sex. The male form,

feeling threatened by their dominance, has been removed.

Winterson explores sexuality; in today's society, women are

still subjected to being only noticed as sex objects used for

men's pleasure. Winterson reveals this through Ron Lord's

Character in the novel with his invention of sexbots, which,

to him, will replace women in general. The way Ron Lord

identifies women is that they are here on this planet for

sexual pleasure, not intellectual interaction. Winterson

explores Gender with Ry, who is a transgender person in

the novel, exploring her identity and her sexuality with her

relationship with Victor, the way her gender is portrayed to others and the way Victor sees her as "delicious new

data"(Winterson 123).

Sexbots in Winterson's novel replace women's

sexuality. Ron Lord is creating a sexbot to return women

for sexual gratification and males. Comparing Ron Lord

and Lord Byron in the book shows they both think similarly

when Lord Byron dismisses Claire as he says, "We four in

our watery world. Five said, Clarie. I forgot said Byron"

(Winterson 10). This informs the reader that Claire was not

counted as an equal within the group, which only named

Mary Shelley, Lord Byron, Polidori, and Percy Shelley. The

only reason Claire was partly recognised was for Lord

Byron's sexual pleasure. That is the only thing Claire was

counted for, similar to a robot that Ron Lord is creating a

women robot for sexual pleasure to give to men. Ron's

outlook is that women are replaceable as they only have

one purpose, so why occupy oneself interacting with an

actual human woman when a robot can give you the exact

needs and desires? Ron states, "Renting gives you all the pleasure and none of the problems". This reveals that a sexbot can be rented, and once you are done using it, return it like it was nothing. Winterson shows us that women are disposable like robots; you can trade her in for a newer model once finished. He is taking away a woman's sexuality by replacing it with a robot that can be commanded by the male on how to act and sexually express their desires instead of an actual woman who chooses how to express herself with her sexuality. In the novel, Ry displays a gender and sexuality entanglement with Victor about her gender and sexuality.

Winterson shows contrasting lives, which include an imagined Mary Shelley, a young transgender person named Ry (Mary), and a recognised artificial intelligence professor called Victor Stein, into an exploration of love, time, and space. There is a love story between Dr Ry Shelley and Professor Stein, an entanglement of fascination with Ry on Victor's side of the story and a wanting of trust

and love with Victor on Ry's side. Winterson portrays that

with Ry, there is no labelling of her gender; she feels

comfortable in her skin. Victor automatically thinks of Ry

as a male. It is only when they are alone together in the

Sonoran desert that Victor realises who Ry is. " he is not

afraid of the scars or their bumpy beauty. To me they are

beautiful. A mark of freedom".(Winterson 120). Ry

apprises Victor that she is a woman and a man in her

preferred body. Doing what she has done brings her nearer

to herself, and she is happy. Ry falls in love with Victor's

fascination with her. Nonetheless, Victor is intrigued by the

idea of Ry because she is a hybrid. Ry is comfortable about

her gender choice and expressing her sexuality. It is only

when Victor says " I love you" (Winterson 153) that

Winterson shows that Ry is scared: "I want to trust him. I

do not trust him" (Winterson 153)—not feeling safe around

Victor, knowing that he only loves the idea of her. She is

choosing to intervene in one's evolution, accelerating the portfolios of possibilities. This attracts Ry, making her excited and enthralled but still not trusting herself around Victor. Victor, a professor in control of what he creates, feels lost and uncertain about Ry, reminding the reader that human relationships and all the accompanying emotions can never be replicated. Sexuality is a person's choice to explore and give, never to be replaced or should ever be replaced by a robotic.

Winterson does not appreciate labels, and she is right; labelling oneself to a particular form restricts that individual from being themselves. In the novel, when Ron Lord encounters Ry, he presumes that the name is short for Ryan and is shocked to find out that it is, in fact, short for Mary. Ry is trying to explain it to Ron Lord, which is interesting in that Winterson shows that explaining your choice of gender to others can be complex and fascinating based on the way others react. Take Ron Lord, for example.

He falls silent, trying to process what Ry has told him. All humans process information at different speeds and levels. This makes the reader think machines are easier to deal with as if you feed them the information that "I am now a man, although I was born a woman, it would not slow up its processing speed". (Winterson 83). Ron is still trying to get around the idea that Ry is transgender and talking about sexbots and that they are narrow-goal robots, and this is what men want. Ry tells him it is not what I wish; Ron looks at Ry with even more doubt and dismay and asks Ry has got a dick. Ry tells him no, and Ron fawns her off, saying, "You are not a bloke". (Winterson 85). In other words, what do you know? It has nothing to do with you as you are not in a proper gender disposition; looking at Ry like the stupidest thing he has ever seen, Winterson is trying to convey to the reader that you have to be a particular gender form to have opinions about things that you should not be allowed to as you are not in that gender form, so you do not know anything. Ron believes you cannot be both if you are a woman or a man. His invention of sexbots is that a robotic sex toy of the female form can replace women. You are supplying men with their sexual needs without having to interact in a conversation with an actual human being.

Men still use the word of God to justify their right to discipline by physical force a wife who is not subordinate. Some battered women continue to accept such abuse because they believe it is a husband-sanctioned 'right and duty'. Winterson shows this behaviour when Ry gets attacked for being the person she wants to be. That even though she fought her attacker, he felt like it was his right to do what he did. Ry escaped, and outside at the wall, she slid down. "And I do not report it because I cannot stand the leers and the jeers and fears of the police. And I cannot stand the assumption that somehow I am the one at fault" (Winterson 244). Winterson is reaching the reader through her novel by expressing that men have the right to do what they want when they want. Making women, even those in transgender form, feel small and invisible, and nobody will listen to them or hear their cries. Men tend to be more powerful than women, and losing this power is upsetting for the male race. Males are inclined to feel more dominant as a gender race; having these sexbots is a form of keeping their control over women and making them feel as powerful as a man is supposed to be.

Winterson opens the reader's eyes to women taking control of themselves, not constricted or confined by gender roles but how they feel like the person within themselves—exploring their sexuality at their level and pace and how it makes them feel. Winterson shows that some, like Ron Lord, are frightened of real women, which results in creating sexbots to boost the male ego by degrading the human form of a woman. The novel explores sexuality and gender in a way that captivates the readers and shows that artificial intelligence is a male-dominated

market. Women get replaced by robots and are told what to

do and how to do it. "Gender is annoying because it defines

us, so I love the idea of trans people saying, 'I am just not

having it'" (Julia Llewellyn Smith). The novel gives the

reader a new definition of gender and how labelling affects

everyone. If you are happy, should it matter what form you

take? Winterson leaves you questioning the idea of gender

and sexuality and also the way artificial intelligence is

going to take over, replacing the women form in that it will

degrade the way women are seen, and this is not a future

anybody wants their children to grow up in, a society that

men are the dominance figure and women are submissive

forms.

Jane Austen's use of irony in Pride and Prejudice forces readers to make alliances with some characters over others.

By Ashling McGee

Jane Austen's *Pride and Prejudice* uses literary irony throughout the novel. "Irony is a fundamental attitude underlying all of Austen's work".(Sorbo 523). Within the opening chapter of *Pride and Prejudice*, the irony is identified. A truth universally acknowledged is that any man with great wealth and status must seek a wife. Jane Austen's novel was known before publication as "First

Impressions". As readers, we are drawn into first impressions designated to each character portrayed in the novel. This forces the readers to align themselves with certain characters within the novel, especially with the characters Elizabeth and Wickham. Then, in a way forced to loathe certain characters such as Mr Darcy. Supporting the statement that Austen makes readers build alliances with certain characters over others, this was Jane Austen's intention from the beginning to get readers to become immersed with certain characters and make alliances with them but then display to the reader that first impressions can be prejudged. Elizabeth and Darcy recognise this. Elizabeth's prejudgment of Darcy is identified as ironic in that she is quick to judge a man whom she later discovers Darcy to be her equal.

The portrayal of characters allows the audience to become submerged in the novel and are charmed by Elizabeth Bennet. As a character of humour and unconventional values, believing that there is much more than just being married out of a sense of having a wealthy husband who has status within the society in which she lives. The first impression that she acquires from Elizabeth is one of liveliness, carefree spirit and independence. Hence, the reader feels connected with her and falls for her charming characteristics. As with Mr and Mrs Bennet, both are represented ironically. Mrs Bennet is made out to be somewhat eccentric, especially when Mr Bennet has an "odd mixture of quick parts, sarcastic humour". As a husband, he enjoys creating mayhem for his wife, which, in turn, causes Mrs Bennet to lose her last nerve, making her excitable and high-strung. She intends to marry her daughters off when Mr Bingley, a single man of a large fortune, arrives. Telling Mr Bennet, "What a fine thing for our girls".(Austen 3). Mr Bennet's response has been sarcastic: "How can it affect them?".(Austen 3) As if stating a fact, Mrs Bennet says, "You must know that I am thinking of his marrying one of them".(Austen 3). The

satire directed towards Mr Bennet and his wife is

enjoyable to read. Their relationship contributes to the

reader's appreciation for the humoristic characters like Mr

and Mrs Bennet, who are witty and clever.

The first impression that the reader is given of Mr

Darcy is that he is a character who is proud, ignorant in

manners and a most disagreeable person. Elizabeth says, " I

could easily forgive his pride if he had not mortified

mine".(Austen 15). This is when Elizabeth overhears a

conversation between Mr Darcy and his friend Mr Bingley

about how Darcy describes Elizabeth as tolerable, not

handsome enough and in no humour to give any

consequence. Elizabeth's first impression of Darcy is one

where the readers also draw an impression of him. Austen

shows the reader the impression of Mr Darcy; in doing so,

he is prejudged by it. The irony is that most individuals

prejudge other people just by the first impression that is

portrayed. As readers, the novel makes an impression on us in different ways. Characters like Elizabeth and Wickham are characters that readers align with. However, the prejudgement designated to those characters is inaccurate, which is informed to the reader later in the novel. Jane Austen wrote it this way so the reader would automatically ally with the characters she desires to fall in love with. Jane then sets out to make the reader despise other characters by describing their demeanour and how they are portrayed in the novel. Throughout the novel, the reader is drawn in to realise that the characters admired and respected are the characters that should have been less respected and more despised. The novel blinds one initially by colouring perceptions of characters and events. This is Austen's clever way of getting the readers intrigued by making alliances with certain characters and closing their eyes to the proper form or identity they represent in the novel.

The reader can see this with how Wickham was introduced to them, having an acceptable man and gallantry appearance, unlike Mr Darcy, whose appearance is camouflaged by his discourteous demeanour. This, in turn, makes the reader fall for Wickham's captivating behaviour. Elizabeth falls for his charm, believing him to be a man of honour and truth. Austen wants the reader to judge these characters by how she portrays them at the novel's start. Later in the book, the reader discovers the hidden truth beneath each character. It is very clever and intriguing that Austen keeps the reader interested in how the relationships develop between each character. The main attraction in the novel is the growing relationship between Mr Darcy and Elizabeth. Elizabeth is a lively soul, always laughing and somewhat playful; this may have been an influence that drew Darcy's attention towards Elizabeth. Darcy, a man of society, a proud gentleman of wealth, cannot afford to be exuberant. This would be out of character for a man of his societal position. He is seen as a man of great importance and stature in the society that he dwells in. Elizabeth sees Darcy as a man of displeasing manners and no respect for those beneath his status. This first impression of Darcy is what the reader believes, and it is not until Elizabeth is given a letter by Darcy that the change is visible in both characters.

The letter which Elizabeth receives is a turning point within the novel. It gives an insight into Darcy's true character as a man Elizabeth thought had been so vain and proud. Now, she recognises a man of great integrity and family values. First, mistaken impressions come to light when Elizabeth doubts her prejudgment of Darcy, as before, the reader perceived Darcy as a wealthy aristocratic class man, overly proud and conscious of his social status. His demeanour and how he treated those of less stature in society made Darcy disagreeable—still, his real character forms mainly within Elizabeth's letter from Darcy.

Elizabeth, a confident, moral, and sharp-witted person, helps her rise above the spiteful society that she dwells in; tending to judge hastily, she is now faced with something unexpected with the perusal of the letter she received. Even though when Elizabeth turns Darcy down on his first marriage proposal, he still treats her gently, although his pride is wounded. The letter manifests his genuine, honest feelings, even by delivering the letter in person, showing how he truly feels for Elizabeth. Darcy sets his heart on explaining the wrong picture of him that Elizabeth has drawn. After reading the letter, Elizabeth feels ashamed at how she judged Darcy. At this moment, she sees a man of great honour and respect, feeling differently about herself now with conflicted feelings. Adoration now opened on both sides. Darcy identifies the way his behaviour and approach towards others can create misjudgement from others. Here and now, Darcy overcomes his pride with the help of Elizabeth, and Elizabeth now overcomes her prejudice against other people through the letter she receives from Darcy. "Elizabeth thinks for a time that her wrong version has cost her a perfect mate and a great house, crucial things for a young lady in that society".(Tanner 112). Beginning now to make sense that Darcy was precisely the man who, in character and strength, would suit her, a union that would be compelled to their advantage. "How despicably have I acted! she cried; I, who have prided myself on my discernment!... Till this moment I never knew myself."(Austen 144). The letter changed everything for both the characters within the novel and the readers, who are now surprised by the revelation of Elizabeth reciting the letter. It was a clever ploy by Austen and showed that, as readers, we prejudge and attach ourselves to characters by how an author writes and describes them to the audience.

There are at least two different kinds of characters within the novel: those who are entirely determined by their roles, even disoriented by them. Then, some can distinguish their roles without losing consciousness of what they are executing. How the language is used within the novel can be noticed in a form where they cannot speak and think outside their specific social circumstances. Elizabeth's and Darcy's matching of wits is a wrestle for control of the narrative. A defining moment in this struggle is the morning after when Darcy delivers the letter to Elizabeth. As soon as the letter is read, Darcy drowns out all of Elizabeth's thoughts; this controls the narrative for the following pages of the novel. Darcy recovers his story and manages its clarification in a struggle for literary dominance. The irony is that Austen made the reader from the very beginning fall deeply in love with Elizabeth's character and her ideal of allying with her, and in doing so, makes the reader take a dislike to Darcy by the way Austen created his character that he was flawed and of lousy demeanour. It is, however, ironic, reading into the novel when Elizabeth receives the letter, how not only did her perception of Darcy change, but the reader's perception also changed. Austen set about portraying Darcy as a gentle, kind, and valued gentleman, unlike the character prejudged at the novel's beginning.

Austen's use of irony was very clever and captured the reader's attention, wanting them to delve into this world of ancient England, of courtship and of men of wealth and women seeking a husband for status and comfortable living with the society they dwell in. Some characters, especially Elizabeth, yearned for a match to call her equal and whom she loved, not just for their wealth or stature in life. Austen sets forth to capture the reader and make them see how their first impressions of characters are perceived. Prejudgment is in everyone who reads the novel, and it does not always hold its value. There is a point within the book where Austen sets out by Elizabeth's distinctive words spoken after she notices that her pride and prejudice steered her in her first attempt, to the misreading of Darcy's letter: "'Till this moment, I never knew myself'".(Austen 144). This shows the reader's reality contrasted through language. Both characters, Darcy and Elizabeth, are proud and cynical of each other; Elizabeth judges Darcy purely on his demeanour, and her first impression of him blinds her to who he is. Darcy sees Elizabeth as a woman of wildness and laughter and someone below his social status. Austen characterises the novel on first impressions and irony. It shows the reader that prejudgement is not always the best way to determine a person's disposition in life. Using sarcasm in the novel makes the reader fall in love with certain characters and invest in them, and then Austen turns it around. The reader is left in astonishment and wonder as the characters begin to show their true identity, leaving the readers speechless and in some way ashamed of the way that they prejudged those characters with whom they aligned themselves. This makes the audience aware that most people prejudge someone before knowing the natural person beneath their disguise. One of Austen's notable

progressiveness is her sense that human events always

occur in a temporal context. As stated earlier, Jane Austen

intended to get the reader to become immersed in certain

characters and make alliances with them, only to be

confronted with the fact that first impressions can be

prejudged.

Slavery and Dehumaninastion through Literary Work

By Ashling McGee

Dehumanisation is a constant, vicious cycle that people live with daily. In many forms, dehumanising a person is stripping away their right to live freely by suppressing their lives, not allowing them to live life on their terms. Their souls are taken away and are suppressed to live by another person's authority and converted into a colonised culture by removing their own. The colour of a person's skin is how one can dehumanise a person. The 'White' people are blinded as some continue to use the word 'Black or Nigger'

and even the word 'Redskin', knowing that it hurts the

person's feelings. It dehumanises those with different

cultures or skin colours, implying that some races are pure

and others are insignificant. Colonisation became a way of

dehumanisation as it pushed those like the native Indians

out of their land into reservations to live in poverty. Those

of coloured skin became enslaved people under the control

of White society. This piece will focus on two works of

literature, 'Huckleberry Finn' and 'Ceremony.' This

literature shows a journey down the Missouri River, giving

insight into dehumanisation. It also shows how alienated a

native Indian is made to feel dehumanised and out of place.

Twain exposes the sanctimony of slavery in his work,

'Huckleberry Finn.' He does this by demonstrating how

racism perverts the tyrants as much as the ill-treated. Some

critics of both races discussed the involvement of White

fantasy when talking about Jim's character and his

relationship with Huck when travelling down the Missouri River together. In particular, Harold Beaver and Forrest Robinson discuss the misty-eyed naivete of White readers who take Jim's fondness for Huck at face value and are ignorant that Jim has his escape plan, and Huck threatens these plans. (Alberti, 921.) Huck's father dehumanises him by beating him, making him feel useless and worthless as a person. He comes from a low-level White society, is not educated, and is left alone to defend himself. When others try to make him more civilised, like when "Miss Watson would say, 'Do not put your feet up there, Huckleberry; and do not scrunch up like that, Huckleberry – set up straight; and pretty soon she would say, 'Do not gap and stretch like that, Huckleberry, - why don't you try to behave?''. (Twain, 4). Huck felt out of place within this colonised society. He resisted the schooling and teachings as his loneliness from society and his doubtfulness of the world around him made him scared, wanting independence and yearning for the

company of someone, and he found that with Jim.

Twain reveals a father-son connection between Huck and

Jim. However, that love is fractured because racism is still

an issue as Huck's conscience begins to waver, realising

the actions for stealing a person who is the property of a

slaveholder. Jim is a gentle, kind man helping Huck as they

travel, but in reality, Jim is in some ways using Huck as a

means towards freedom both as a political and social status,

using Huck and the boat to cross into a 'Free' state.

Huck begins to see an unstable sense of justice, which he

encounters within society, that terrible acts go

undisciplined, yet piety crimes such as drunken insults can

lead to executions. Sherburn's speech to a lynch mob

shows this view of society. "If any real lynching is going to

be done, it will be done in the dark, Sothern fashion; and

when they come, they will bring their masks and fetch a

man along." (Twain 139). Sherburn states he is safe as daylight, and the crowd is a cowardly and pathetic crowd of humanity. A man of his stature is free and clear, and nobody has the courage or willpower to do anything to stop him. Another form of dehumanisation is the people's fear of a man of great wealth and power in society. He has control, and they are just weak, cowardly people under his command. It shows how Huck is not accessible or can escape the social and practical limitations that suppress him as a victim of abuse and vulnerability to the society in which he lives. There is a connection between Twain's work and Silko's as they both show vulnerability and racism in which the White people destroy the native Indians' culture through colonisation and skin colour.

Silko states that the native people felt out of place as racism alienated them from the Whites. The colonisation of the native Indians dehumanised the natives, making them feel inferior and forcing them to live on the Land inhabitable to farm. The natives are seen in two ways: they served their country during the war and were respected as they aided their American government. When the war ended, they were rendered useless and disposable, and their place within society was not deemed fittable as Tayo perceives: "I am a half breed. I will be the first to say it. I will speak for both sides. The first time you walked down the street in Gallup or Albuquerque, you knew. Do not lie. You knew right away. The war was over; the uniform was gone. All of a sudden, that man at the store waits on you last and makes you wait until the White people buy what they want." (Silko, 39). After receiving medals of honour, they are now dehumanised by the White people disrespecting them and not acknowledging them for their part during the war. Tayo felt alone and without a place of belonging in American and Indian cultures. His soul is lost, and he needs to find his place in the world. He wanted to feel a sense of belonging with the White people, not blaming them for taking the native's Land and enjoying

White people's friendship. Forgetting about his native

culture as he was colonised into a White society and lost

his native heritage. The term breed that Tayo uses gives

insight into how people treat others in a society dominated

by their race. Two worlds are pulling Tayo apart, and he

has no place either, as people from both sides do not accept

him as he is of mixed culture and does not fit into any

society.

 The dehumanisation he feels is inferiority, and the

prejudicious experiences that he encounters forbid him

from any joy in his life. The apparent form of racism is that

White people believe the native Indians are a form of

property. Silko's story tells us, "White people who

dedicated their lives to helping the Indians these people

urged her to break away from home. She was excited to see

that despite the fact she was an Indian, the White men

smiled at her from their cars".(Silko, 63). White people

believed that they were helping a young, impressible girl be more civilised in their society by dressing like them and conforming to their world. However, they stripped her down, making her more fitting to belong in their culture, removing her native heritage, and making her feel alone and ashamed of her people and White people like a monster with two sides within her separating her dividing her into two dehumanising her to the point of not knowing where she belongs anymore. Silko displays a recurring problem in today's society as people are trapped between two worlds due to the colour of their skin and mixed descent and feel no sense of belonging, no matter how hard they try.

In writing this piece, one thing came into clear focus: dehumanising a person or a nation recurs daily. The colonisation of American Land by White people destroyed the beauty and heritage of the people that already existed there. Many different cultures fight to belong and live in a colonised society, but it is a daily struggle for those trying to belong in both worlds; Twain's 'Huckleberry Finn' displayed how Whites controlled the narrative of those bound by slavery and those trying to free themselves from a world of pain and wanting to live a free life of their choosing. Silko's 'Ceremony' is similar to Twain's as racism and colonisation are factors, and the integration of the Whites and the native Indians and those called 'half breeds' born of two identities struggling to find a place they fit. One could question the American saying, 'Land of freedom and opportunity. Who are they talking about? Who is it accessible to, and what opportunities are there? These questions people could ponder, but it is the White people's world of freedom and possibilities in some ways. Other races and cultures have to fight for their freedom and belonging in a colonised America, where some feel isolated and dehumanised in a society that now exists.

<u>Self-Reliance through Literature</u>

by Ashling McGee

Defying Self-reliance is trying to define yourself. Self-reliance is vital for a person to conform to the idea of working to nonconformity. Emerson believes the truth is within oneself to adhere to institutions like religion. Emerson was a transcendentalist who accepted ideas not as religious beliefs but as a way of understanding life relationships. He discusses movements like the protestant reformation and the American Revolution as ways toward self-reliance, a form of human freedom. Individualism is superior to the mass of people. Emerson sees that one person's views or visions are far more effective and can be seen further than a scene of several people. This means one person's view can be more effective than a collaboration of a group's view.

Emerson's powerful words make one think about how, as a person, you can be an individual and be self-reliant without being part of an institution following the norm like everyone else. Some are too scared to take the chance and would instead follow the norm, but at the end of the day, your choice matters, and you should do it willingly and not be forced by politics, religion, or peer pressure. You matter, and what you decide should count as it is what you want, not someone else's beliefs but yours. In Emerson's essay, there is a tension between self and society. He never really shows how he sees a society of self-reliant individuals; if possible, he intends for evolution to surface.

Society is something that a person must deal with, and escaping is not a solution for Emerson. "Society is a wave. The wave moves onward, but the water of which it is composed does not". This shows how, in some ways, society can change but remain the same. As the person who speaks out and the nation listens, so do their experiences after they die. It can leave ripple effects that are carried on from century to century. One person's views and ideas from the past can still affect some people today and are willing to change nonconformity. Protestantism influenced American literature in the movements after transcendentalism and ancestry, which is evident in how literature participated in the moral lives of Americans during and after the Civil War.

Self-reliance today can be seen through the lives of refugees. Seeking to improve their lives as they cannot count on relief, they try to be self-reliant, fleeing conflicts and violations of human rights, which shows courage in their efforts to survive in host countries. In South Africa, refugees enjoy freedom of movement and have various legal rights but still feel vulnerable, resulting in exposed dignity. Seen as parasites, the locals think they are deprived of multiple services, and refugees are enjoying living off the fruits of their labour and struggle for freedom. Most refugees use the help they receive as newcomers; they try to establish themselves by rebuilding their lives and becoming self-reliant.

Being self-reliant improves their livelihoods and reduces their vulnerability and dependence on assistance. It is hard as they compete for jobs the locals will be going for, and of course, the locals will always get top priority. Some Congolese refugees launched the vision of the development of FIZI. This mobilises African communities living in South Africa by helping them find work and adapt to an unknown culture. This is great; they know they are not alone in their struggles and that others are like them. This can help change their destiny. If South Africa could come to this state of mind, the country could become more than a place to stay but a place of opportunity where refugees can find fulfilment.

Refugees migrate as their lives do not lead to a life of dignity and self-worth where they live. Their emigration is for freedom without being reduced to nothingness. Facing specific challenges like being called parasites or subhuman by locals is a struggle for refugees. Still, they show great courage in the first place for leaving the abusive environment where they once lived. Self-reliance has come forward as theory has been put into practice by these refugees trying to be self-reliant and choosing to leave a life they knew, start over, and make a new life worth living. Emerson has opened the minds of so many and is still incorporated into today's society as some strive to be self-reliant and change to make a better life and help others do the same.

Past and future theories can unite and form a bond that makes everyone living anywhere in the world stand up, be noticed, and fight for what they want and the rights they deserve. As centuries move, those significant figures that have passed, we learn something as individuals and grow with their ideas. It may be long forgotten, but it is still in your mind, and it only takes one person to stand up and say something, and people will listen. Powerful speeches come and go. How people implement them continues and passes from one era to the next. In today's society, it can be challenging for some to change as you have settled into a culture where you feel you belong, but are you happy? That is something that you have to consider and decide for yourself. Like the refugees, it takes courage to go forward and venture into a new and different place, and trying to be self-reliant is a struggle. I do not think Emerson ever said it would be easy. However, when challenged, you can prove yourself wrong.

Feminism with Ngozi Adichie is seen through Beyonce's Song Flawless.

By Ashling McGee

Looking at how women were judged and treated long ago, in some ways, it is carried out today. Gender where men were "masculine", and their characteristic patterns were associated with aggressiveness, rationality, and assertiveness. The women were "feminine" and had personalities such as gentleness, sensitivity, and intuitiveness. These gender roles translated into specific patterns of taught behaviour and feeling. This became the order of things: men worked while the women cleaned the house. The male dominated the woman. It still happens today more with the older generation of people from generations of being brainwashed or taught that is the social order of things. However, the newer generation is more outspoken, changing how women can be more self-reliant and open. Even men are changing their views as society begins to be more accessible and more open to change. You have those that society empowers, those who have been privileged, and then there are those oppressed. In Beyoncé's song "Flawless" featuring Chimanda Ngozi Adichie, you can see women with different views on feminism. They both speak out about feminism and oppression; the video shows us a statement of Gender, Race and class. It shows multiculturalism and not judging a person because of their skin tone and putting them in a group to which you think they belong, like a group of skin colour or a white power supremacist.

In the early nineteenth century, married women had no legal identity apart from their husbands. This was known as coverture, which meant no woman had the right to write a will or own property after their husband's death and custody of their children went to the father. Things have changed, but women still fight for the right to belong in a male-dominated world. In the song "Flawless", the line "We teach girls to shrink themselves". This means this is the society women live in. Make yourself small and have ideas but not too many. Strive for success but do not overpower the men; do not challenge patriarchy. The song shows that by fighting for it, you can be a queen and have it all: wealth, jewels and a husband who makes you feel good about yourself. Not to be put down and kept in line like a society group you should belong to, like "a wife's only worthwhile achievement is to make her husband happy". (Germaine Greer p307). The wife's job was to make their husband happy as he had more important things to do than make her happy. Things are beginning to change within society, which has much to do with women speaking out about feminism. They do this through media platforms such as music, literature and public speaking. We hear and see this through the song "Flawless".

Beyoncé and Chimamanda Ngozi Adichie collaborate and have different views on expressing feminism. Adichie respects and admires Beyoncé, as there is more than one way to be a feminist. Beyoncé's feminism gives space to the necessity of men. In contrast, Adichie's feminism argues that giving men this space takes away the attention that should be given to women since it is about women's liberation. Adichie explains how men are at the centre of women's lives. This is where the problem is in the feminism expressed by Beyoncé; she still uses her body as an admiration for men to look upon, and in turn, it could be seen that it is what men want in a woman: beauty over brains, you could say. However, Adichie puts women first, and that is what the future of feminism should be about. Turning our focus on women and seeing value in ourselves shows our diversity and not being identified as men but about ourselves as women. These two women coming together show their respective differences regarding feminism and how diverse it is and put into action.

It can also be seen through the "Flawless" video how society is affected by different power systems such as patriarchy and white supremacy. You are categorised into a specific group by looking different and being different due to skin colour and appearance. Within the video, you see skinheads who would be associated with a white power supremacist whose race is superior, but just because you have a skinhead does not mean you are a part of that group. Judged by looks and colour and not by the person you are, society locks you into a particular group, and you are then all judged according to the group society sees you in. In a white supremacist society, people of colour do not have race-based institutional power. Being white and poor is different to been black and poor. White people have support network resources to help them by using these to gain employment, and white people are more likely to be the interviewer as they hold an executive position, so they are the same race as you. This gives you more of an advantage of gaining that position towards a black person. A black person does not have access to these resources and is subjected to racial prejudice as those who hold the power are of a white race. It is doubtful that black people would get the job position when applying in a white-dominated area. However, the video shows Beyoncé stating her presence of wealth and how she worked hard to earn what she has but look at me, here I am. Do not judge by the colour of your skin or how you look. Everyone is their personal. The line "I am so crown bow down, bitches" means here I stand in front of you like royalty. I made it to the top. I do not take any crap and fight for what I believe, so bow down and respect me.

In today's society, the likes of "Flawless" how icons like Beyoncé portray a version of feminism which states outlooks on religion, culture and sexual identity. In some cases, a woman can still be placed inside a box where she can be a sexual object for men's gratification, but not wise as well. Women are trying to break these norms set by gender by expressing themselves and showing their views through feminist activism. You are reflecting on the reality of their own lives and seeking to rectify injustices that have been continuing by historic patriarchally-led hegemonic structures. These feminist activists continuously emerge as women fight the changing social and political landscapes around them. McIntosh tells us that being a white person, you are taught about racism, which is something that puts others at a disadvantage. In some ways, being classed into white privilege, you are protected from distress and even violence. The colour of your skin does this as it is the norm or way of life in which you are born. As a person, you are not racist, but still, you are granted liberties which you may not even notice or see as being part of the colour of your skin. You walk confidently, knowing you will be accepted, but some are weighed down with hostility and must fight to get where they wish to go. "Being of the main culture, I could also criticise it fairly freely." (Peggy McIntosh p74). I have been blind to other groups who are made uncomfortable and non-important. The "Flawless" video shows how everyone, no matter what gender, race or group you are put into, is essential. Those should not be judged just by the way they look and act, the colour of their skin or their gender you are. Being privileged does not mean your life is easy, and you did not work hard, but it is easier than others who face difficult obstacles they encounter and must overcome them. Society does not change overnight. It takes time and people to speak out, keep speaking and expressing their views, and fight for the change they want. It is by others listening and opening their mind to opinions blocked by a generation of being put into a group that society saw you deemed necessary to belong in. Stepping out of this familiar norm and expressing your views shows strength and self-reliance, and it is possible to change how we see society even if we intentionally judge each other within ourselves.

Perception of Race through Robin Diangelo's Work

By Ashling McGee

The perception of race is everywhere, from the outside and inside of a person. The concept of race has been inescapable from the beginning of time. Is it fair to say that this has changed over the centuries? Perhaps not, but to this day, racism and discrimination continue. One can remove the words from any discourse about racism, but racism is still embedded within the fabric of our society. Some whites believe that racism is a thing of the past and that it is best not to acknowledge it. In the present, racial differences between whites and people of colour exist in every institution across society today and are increasing instead of decreasing.

Suppose you consider the slogan "Black Lives Matter", which is circulated across society. In that case, this slogan is connected to the culture of white privilege, which continues despite the forbidding of open expression of racial feelings.

The primary assumption of whiteness is that the definition of whites is the rule for humanity, and those of coloured skin is a deflection from the rule. Those of us with white skin forget or do not recognise whiteness as a separate state of existence which could impact a person's life and perception. White dominance is influential mainly in countries with a history of colonialism by Western nations. In all fairness, that is most of the world, which has been at some point colonised or controlled by white people. The white authority has shaped a system of European domination. It has brought into existence whites and those of colour, imposing white ideological conditioning on non-whites. This unnamed political system is invisible, and the white's power is taken from it; everything within its society is taken for granted.

The stories whites tell through the likes of media impact how people judge and see the world. Each generation of people is influenced and thinks this is the norm or normality of life. Children are brought up today and learn not to be racist, and all lives matter, but still, this unnamed system of invisibility remains within each white person. Cultural information, including stories, images, omissions, and silence, is passed down from one person or group to the next and from generation to generation. This white racial frame includes negative understandings of non-whites and positive understandings of whites and their institutions. One can understand why the slogan "Black Lives Matter" is so meaningful; as we say, all lives matter retrospectively. Are we just saying the lives of people within the norm of our society matter? This imprint of what a normal society should be is enforced by an unnamed society of invisibility where everything is taken for granted, and even though some may

take a stand against racism and fight for the rights of people

with coloured skin, does it affect or change how society

lives?

As children, they are curious and ask questions. In a

society where a child sees something different or someone

different, they will be interested. They may loudly shout in

the middle of a store, "That person is black", and as a white

mother, you "Shush your child", as a feeling of

embarrassment and anxiety overcome you. The question is,

why did you Shush your child? Was it as it was impolite or

just the norm of the society in which you were brought up

in. They pretend you do not notice what you have done as if

making it disappear. Would the white mother have the same

reaction if the child shouted " big White person"? Unlike the

other statement, there would not be a feeling of

embarrassment or anxiety. You would laugh about it and

move along. This shows aspects of white children's racial

socialisation. The child learns that talking about race is restricted. They also know that a person's differences should go unnoticed. The children are then brought up in a world where it is the norm to do these things, which is how society exists.

Even though society is evolving and things are beginning to change, some things remain the same as the way white privilege continues to exist within Western countries. The schools you attend, the jobs you get, the neighbourhood you live in, and even the treatment you receive from those in power, like the police force and the courtroom. All these represent a white privilege in society which continues today. The concept is that a neighbourhood with more people of colour causes a rise in criminal activity, so the home value will drop and be known as a bad neighbourhood. It will deter whites from living there and wanting to live in a better neighbourhood, meaning a neighbourhood of white people where everything is accepted and you follow the norm of society. Let us take, for example,

a crime in which a white person and a person of colour are

involved and which one receives the worst punishment. In

most cases, the white person will receive a slap on the wrist

and maybe a fine to pay. The person of colour will be the one

that the judge makes an example of. They would be brought

to court and, in front of a white judge system, exploited and

sent to prison for a crime that was committed by both a

person of colour and a white person. The media would

manipulate the story, twisting the facts and making it about

how the person of colour was the main initiator and that the

white person was in fear for their life and went along with it.

It explodes out of proportion, and the focus is on the people

of colour as the white's participation fades into the

background. This, again, is a statement of white privilege

and white dominance that all people of colour will be treated

like this, placing fear within the people of colour and

conforming to how society works being colonised by white

people. The whites who do feel sorry for the people of colour do not speak up. They stay silent and ignore what is happening and do not question their guilt. "leaving it to people of colour to tackle racial issues, offloading the tensions and social dangers of speaking openly onto them" This shows why they fight for justice and why the slogan "Black Lives Matter" is essential. It is to get the attention of those who are listening but not acting to do something and speak out, showing that things can change if only you open your mind and mouth to stop the invisible system still in today's society.

A life of independence through James Joyce's work 'A Portrait of the Young Artist as a Young Man'

By Ashling McGee

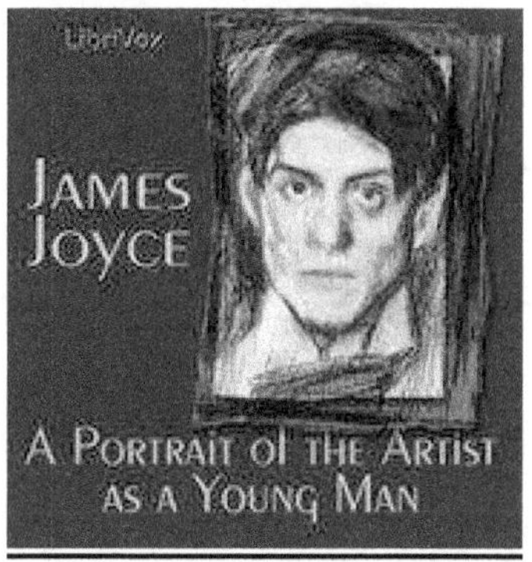

A Portrait of the Artist as a Young Man narrates the story of James Joyce. He portrays himself through the novel as a man named Stephen Dedalus. This character within the book is James Joyce's alter ego, a mythical representation of himself. Stephen wants a life that is full and not confined by the boundaries of family, religion and the Country of Ireland in which he lives. Joyce sets about sending Stephen on two pathways: order and religious structure, the other filled with the unknown of curiosity and freedom. Stephen searches for an ideal self which will replace what he believes is his shallow, authentic self. The dominant focus of the novel is life from childhood to adulthood, along with the continuous presence of the sacramental cycle. This confronts the complex relationship that Joyce himself had with the Catholic church.

Throughout the novel, Joyce's writing manifests imagery and references regarding the development of the religious sacraments. It displays how a man's life goes through a transformation throughout the book of him turning against religion, defying it but returning to his faith again at one stage and to a newfound state of devotion to beauty and becoming an artistic talent. Joyce does not show a baptismal service but displays it to the reader through imagery shown through Stephen's vision of a "sea of waves, long dark waves rising and falling under the moonless night". An interpretation of this could be connected to baptismal service as the sea represents the bowl of water in which your head is placed. The rising and falling of water represents water being taken from the bowl, and it falls gently over your head; the moonless night could represent the shadow figure of the priest blocking the light as he stands over you. The death of Charles Stewart Parnell, referred to in the novel, is what Joyce shows as being pushed and pulled between rebellion and obedience regarding religion. The life Joyce depicts is structured around the tension between life as a priest and an artist. This life and its relationship with the church is one of complexity.

The idea of following a life without religion is full of colour and wonder, whereas a life of holy order to Joyce represents a feeling of coldness and decay. A man struggling with two identity paths sees him reject his faith and turn to a life of rebellion and exile when he is older. When he was younger, he felt a sense of restraint by the pressure of religion growing up in a Catholic household. With an ambition for freedom and independence, Joyce states an insufficiency of self-awareness and freedom in his life connected by guilt detachment and a sense of awakening. Joyce's use of a skull image is in connection with the priesthood, which can symbolise death and coldness. The idea of becoming a priest, a lifeless soul and a faceless person behind a mask, just cold and has no light or beauty surrounding them. "He opened the theatre door and halted in the chilly grey light that struggled through the dusty windows," describing a poorly lit room, dark and displeasing with no colour or bright light that shines upon you. The rejection of the priesthood is now more evident and drawn to Joyce's mind as there is no beauty within it; it is unappealing and cold.

The rejection of the holy order "Drifts away from the intellectual to the purely physical". I am fascinated by the seduction of prostitutes, as this is the unknown and a defiance against religion. It is the sinful way of disobeying order, knowing it is wrong and aware of it, having no instincts to confess. Pride of sin steers away from the church, and Catholic laws suggest the forgotten of a sacramental structure. If one confesses, they are granted penance and forgiveness, and those who sin can still turn to a path of righteousness. Joyce illuminates the contemplation of confession and seeking atonement. Ashamed of their sins, he struggles with the words in the confessional but does confess and receive a pardon from God as "He knelt to say his penance, praying in the corner of the dark nave and his prayers ascended to heaven from his purified heart like perfume streaming upwards from a heart of white rose". This could be interpreted as a symbol of his first confession in quite a long time, a feeling of shame and an acceptance of God and the sacramental structure in some ways. This shows his respect for religion and willingness to atone for his sins. Still yearning, though, for a life of beauty and not being constrained by order and structure. He is struggling to find a way to live his life to the fullest of his potential.

A person defying the Catholic church can turn their soul into rock growing up. The disorderly life of which was received from their father. A father figure in which a man is lost in nostalgia is used to symbolise the burden placed upon a family as they grow up. A trip to Cork in which a father and son journey displays a picture of a man who drinks so much and who is in ruins, a tragic figure of a man with pride in tradition but unable to hold on and instead drinks it away with alcohol. This father figure represents a lifeless soul, loveless and cold. Associating him with church tradition and order with no life of colour or beauty, just a grey steel and cold surface that Joyce is fighting so hard to leave and turning to a life of beauty and intrigue, resisting the priesthood and church order, leaving Ireland in pursuit of a life of fulfilment. Choosing to be an artist is an escape from rules and regulations. They are isolating away as the feelings of guilt that we seem unable to accept others. The acceptance and rejection of the sacramental structure that

Joyce took in the forms of baptism, communion, and confession are depicted throughout the novel through references and images. His rebellion against these and the struggles that lead him to turn his back on it all, leaving Ireland and everyone and everything behind, shows a man trying to find his way in the world and not be ruled by what structure to follow.

Religion and nationality made Joyce feel ashamed and restrained him against a free life of fulfilment. He concludes by living a life of silence through art, not serving anything in the world he belongs to. The idea of Joyce as a young person to the man he has become feels betrayed by all; this gives a new path to follow and walk along in which there is a life of artistic talent through a life of silence. During his journey towards this new pathway, he encountered obstacles that led to betrayal, guilt and shame—losing one's identity. This man struggled with his identity and yearning for freedom and is now endowed with self-hatred. This has been placed upon Joyce by his family and church. "This hatred emerges when his ideal self overcomes his real self". The struggle to find a self-identity left Joyce a man with self-hatred, a life of silence through artistic expression. Not fully an artist but a figure of one leaving behind a life of structure, replacing it with a sense of self-hatred. This is an accurate figure of an artist. A man taking control of his destiny and life shows strength and signifies the beginning of a life as an artist. Joyce's alter ego, depicted throughout the novel, gives an in-depth analysis of the faithful James Joyce. A man struggling with faith in Ireland during Protestant and Catholic religious feuds. These are confusing times for any young person to go through. Do you honour the traditions you were brought up with or rebel against and decide for yourself what you want from life? Leaving everyone behind to find oneself can be complex. However, leaving shows that he still respects his nation and religion and leaves to find his true path without being confined and restrained in Ireland

and having to live a life he does not wish to and feels shame about. Struggling to find a self-identity in a confusing time built around order and structure is hard for anyone to do. It can leave a person, as we see with Joyce, a man filled with self-hatred and loneliness. It is quite like how he looked upon the priesthood, but he still has beauty within himself through his artistic expression.

Structural Racism in Toni Morrison's book "Beloved"

By Ashling McGee

Toni Morrison's novel 'Beloved' is a powerful betrayal of enslaved people and how they are denied freedom and equality. It shows how they suffered emotionally, physically and psychologically through the African American struggle. It demonstrates how dominant white society governs the black community, denying them to live a life they can call their own. Even after escaping from slavery, they are never free from the dominant white figures who set rules to abide by. They are never free to live with their identity as their skin colour still dehumanises them. The novel has multiple voices which tell the story. It goes from memories like flashbacks and the present, which shape the structure of 'Beloved'. Even from the beginning, the first line, "124 was SPITEFUL"(Morrison 3). A small sentence that is packed with so much. The reader is hit with this from the start: what is 124, a number that can define so much a place, a name, a person's identity? What is it, and why was it spiteful? It intrigues the reader and gets them thinking about what it means. It asks the question of this nasty, cruel number, who or what it is, and how it is so cold. Morrison's characters give us an insight into enslavement and human exploitation, showing how white behaviour and dominance control the lives of African Americans. They have still been influenced by this White superiority even after slavery was abolished. They still live with the horrific tortures and how they affect their lives from moving forward.

The focus of the novel is enslaved people working in an institutionalised system. Morrison bases this on the character Sethe, as she is the one who experiences most of the severe conditions of this system. In this slave system, those exposed to it suffer violence, and brutality, are treated inhumanely like animals, and the women are raped repeatedly. Sethe decides to run from this, trying to give her children a better life, but she can never hide, which drives her to kill her daughter—to her death seemed a better life than slavery as she did not want her children to live that life. The reader feels that Sethe had no other option but that death was a way to free her child from this life of an institution filled with torture and the physical and emotional abuse that went along with it. Slavey causes harmful ramifications for enslaved people as it triggers a reaction to protect. However, in the most severe form, as seen in the novel, Sethe chooses death for her children as a better life than a life of being enslaved. White domination is shown by slavery and racism, which is demonstrated throughout the novel. The Whites have a dominant presence over the Blacks in forms of discrimination and the treatment of enslaved people. Sethe tries to rebuild a life after enslavement. Morrison says, "To Sethe, the future was a matter of keeping the past at bay. She believed the "Better Life" she and Denver were living was not the other one".(Morrison,51). Living this life may have been better than living on the plantation. However, White society still governed it as the house they resided in was owned by a brother and sister of the Bodwin family of White nationality with conditions attached. The Bodwins supplied a life free from slavery and horrific treatment, but all the same, they provided employment and housing, but at what cost? They still dominated the Black community as they had rules of decorum that must be met. The jobs they provided kept those working for them dependent on their authority and offered low wages, so they had no sufficient funds outside the Whites' control. The Bodwin's may have been good people, but they still had this power over the black people and controlled how they lived and what they did. The Character Baby Suggs shows how she did not have an identity as it was stripped away, and she became known as Baby Suggs. She worked for the Bodwins as a domestic worker, doing laundry, as a seamstress, and much more. When she died, she had nothing to her name, not even that, and she describes herself as nothing. This shows us that black people were entitled to nothing, to own nothing, not even a name. They were working hard for very little money, restricting them from making their own life. They could own no property or anything that might give them an independent life outside of white superiority.

Throughout the novel, men and women of colour are dehumanised and degraded into nothing. Women were more at risk, subjected to rape, and always vulnerable to this treatment as they were regarded as insufficient. All black people were treated like animals, and their identity was taken from them as they did not deserve any respect from white society. The black males were subjected to humiliation and more physical abuse. This dehumanised them and made them feel like they were nothing better than animals in a cage

under the Whites' dominant control system. Morrison says,

"The ditches; the one thousand feet of earth five feet deep,

five feet wide, into which wooden boxes have been fitted. A

door of bars you could lift on hinges like a cage opened into

three walls and a roof of scrap lumber and red dirt".(

Morrison 125). This vivid image gives the reader a clear look

at how the enslaved men were treated, locked up like caged

animals conducted by authority, isolating them from any

human interaction through verbal and physical abuse,

resulting in the servitude of black people by the whites. The

most horrific part is when the reader is subjected to the rape

of Sethe on the Plantation by the master, known as a

schoolteacher and his two nephews. The nephews rape her

while her husband is subjected to watching and doing

nothing to save her. This shows their powerlessness; the

husband's manhood is stripped away as he watches what

they do to his wife. Sethe is degraded in the vilest way she could be and used as a playtoy for white men to with as they will. She, as a woman, has nothing to protect her from this life, and the consequence of this leads her to the killing of her daughter as a means of escapism. The Racism shown by the schoolteacher and his nephews is the most undisguised in the novel. This racist act by the schoolteacher and his nephews on the African American enslaved people under his authority on the plantation is because society allows it to happen. It is seen as not punishable. They are allowed to infiltrate these acts as they are done under the institution of slavery, enabling them to behave in this manner towards African Americans.

Both men and women were dehumanised and treated like livestock. Black women were seen as breeders and used to reproduce more enslaved people. This was violated through rape as white men used sexual exploits of black women to increase their profit margin. Even after escaping the plantation, they were still subjected to white domination and treated like servants and objects to be used. This is shown when Sethe has no money to pay for engraving her dead daughter's grave. Her body is used for the payment: "Ten minutes, he said. You got ten minutes, I will do it for free".(Morrison,5). She used her body to pay for seven letters to write on the engraving. She chooses to write BELOVED. She would have gotten more letters if she had given her body over to him for more time. It shows whites' power over blacks as they used their bodies to receive something so small. The novel tells a dark reality with forms of racism and slavery. It tells the reader of the destruction of the cultural identity of those of colour. It shows how African Americans were subjected to racism, sexism and demoralisation, showing an apparent conflict between whites and blacks and that whites are the dominant controllers. Due to their sex and colour, it shows the deprivation of human rights of blacks and the hatred they received and still receive in today's society. Morrison shows how white domination includes socio-cultural and economic aspects, leading to disadvantages and ramifications for the black people who are dominated. We see this in the schoolteacher as he teaches his pupils to list the characteristics of the enslaved people by placing them in specific categories: human and animal. In turn, the teacher leads them to ignore black people's humanity, using their racial aspects against them. This ensures the next generation carries on this racial hate towards those of different coloured skin. The effects of racism are shown throughout the novel as portrayed by victims and the perpetrators by displaying individual types of racism and how these intertwine, creating cultural dominance. The reader sees the interactions between Sethe and different white people, reflecting on her position and where she fits into society. Various white people have other connections with Sethe and different agendas, but they connect and form a foundation of cultural dominance. The Bodwins may feel they are saving the black people and believe they are doing what is best for African Americans.

They are superior to blacks, and blacks need discipline to fit

into society with the white law governing them.

Charles Dickens Oliver Twist, of the criminal underworld and its relation to legitimate society.

By Ashling McGee

Dickens's Novel Oliver Twist conveys injustice within social classes, from upper-class society to the lower class, who commit criminal acts to survive. Oliver Twist is a work of literature that gives those who read it a reality of life lived in London's society during the Victorian Era of the Nineteenth Century. The image that Dickens shows is one of the dark shadows hidden among the society in London. It calls attention to the readers to be part of these feelings that Dickens displays for those who live in poverty, and crime is a means of gaining what they need to survive. There is a social gap between class societies where the upper class sees the lower class as a different race. It is a dark mix of poverty and criminality. Those classed as criminals grab the reader's imagination by the criminal's aspiration to challenge society. Oliver is a victim of society and the legal institution and is a good child trying to survive his harrowing experiences. Oliver is a combination of mixed darkness and normality and a distinct dividing line between poverty and criminality on one hand and normalcy on the other side that can blur disturbingly.

In Dicken's novel, there is an expectation that the higher class deems the lower class as criminals and deviants. Lower-class people turn to stealing and pickpocketing as a means of survival. They are mistreated both emotionally and economically by those upper-class society figures. One of Dickens's most famous quotes is, "Please, Sir, I want some more"(Dickens 12). It shows the preconception against those who are poor, where Oliver's response to asking for more food is pretentious. Like many others, the young boy just wanted another spoonful as he was starving. This states a lack of food and child labour within harsh conditions of the workhouse. The reaction of the fat, healthy man at the workhouse is based on overshadowing social implications and not the actual situation of a malnourished young boy. This highlights that poor people have no right to request or ask of a society that does not contribute to its existence. They want more than they have earned, and the honest, hard-working class has the burden of feeding people experiencing poverty that are classed as nothing but a waste in Victorian high society. Oliver is seen as a criminal in the making with an eagerness beyond his life station. "The boy will be hung" (Dickens 12). This nobody contradicts when it is said that he is classed as the lowest of the low, a pure waste on society that is burdened by hard-working people to be submitted to feed these wretched, poor people. As a punishment, he is put into confinement, and then a note is placed on the gate offering him up as a trade for five pounds to be taken off their hands. Used as a commodity rather than a human being, it shows what society thought of those less fortunate.

Within the Victorian Era, criminals were those of poverty, a stain on society and the other side was wealth and respectability. You were classed into these as if you were a poor person, and you were automatically degraded as a criminal. You were not respected, which drove many to criminal acts to survive, not by choice but as a necessity of the society that you lived in. The legal system used the poor houses and prisons to keep the filth and uncleanness of the streets of London in line with what society deemed proper. The character Fagin is used to show the criminal underworld in London. Fagin uses children as exploitation in a life of criminal acts. Rejecting legal and moral actions, Fagin offers those without a place to stay and food. In return, he exposes them to the world of thievery. Fagin's pickpocketing game where trains these children through a game-like scenario, using it as a tool for them to see if they can do it on the streets and how much they can bring back to him without getting

caught.

When Oliver is faced with doing this game in the

street, he realises what he is about to do. He has a moral

conscience and knows the cost of his actions if he does this.

This, however, does not stop a crowd from chasing him,

believing he is the thief. Society already sees him as poor

and poor, which are classed as one. Everyone in this class of

society is seen as the same whether they do the crime or not.

The issue with London in the 19th century was

unemployment due to the Industrial Revolution, which

brought poverty and homelessness. It led those like Fagin to

take what they wanted as they were already seen as the

lowest to walk the streets. The increase in crime is the

relationship between poverty and unemployment. Those on

the brink of starvation turn to crime to survive. Dickens's

character, Bill Sikes, is the outcome of this system losing all

human kindness as he is so deep in crime in an immoral

society to which he belongs, shaping him to be this person with no compassion and anger all the time. Losing control of the society he lives in, he treats Nancy like he would treat a dog growling at her. She is kind and friendly, but as poverty leads her to a dangerous path of crime and prostitution, she is a good person. Dickens describes her as "Being remarkably free and agreeable in their manner"(Dickens 57). She saves Oliver at a tremendous personal cost, leading to her death at the hands of Sikes. It does show that some can be incorruptible no matter the circumstances of their lives.

Social changes did cause social problems. It creates a specific social class due to living conditions such as poverty. This leads society to turn against those who are down on their luck, classing them as criminals and not respectable enough to fit into a society where wealth is classed as respectable. Separating these two social identities brought high crime in London in the 19th Century. For most, it was a means to survive, not a choice, where workhouses and child labour were seen as a burden on the working class, who had to help those who needed it. They were seen as filth and dirt that needed to be maintained either by the workhouses or the prison. This was a way for societies to control them. The economic and social status were seen as indistinguishably connected to moral character. Those in society saw people experiencing poverty as being vicious. Just because you were poor, you were given the status of being a criminal. Even those who begged were seen as taking fruits from someone else's labour. Some villages had large boards stating, "Warning all persons who begged within the district they would be sent to jail" (Dickens 47). This shows how the law was wrong in being punished because you were hungry. The upper class hide behind this law of government to keep control. Dickens's work brings attention to massive issues that society neglects. This use of London as its setting is authentic and states the impact emotionally and legitimately on the city's problems it has. When Oliver does not regard himself as a thief, it shows how different some can be reformed, unlike Sikes, Fagin and Nancy, who have lived in a world where they know nothing better. Nancy sacrifices herself for Oliver, and instead of taking the opportunity to start fresh somewhere else, she remains, as this is the life she knows, and she knows no other way of living. Society has deemed her this way and that no other life is possible.

There is no escape, which shows the self-esteem issues related to those who turn to criminal acts to survive. They see that once this path is taken, there is no return. Oliver was thrust into this society, and different conclusions in the novel are drawn from societal dogma associated with legal status and economic and social factors that subscribed to their progress. This dividing line between poverty and criminality is blurred by society's desire to protect one's status and reputation. Respectability and those seen as non-respectable just because they are less fortunate are what society deems as proper—using the law and workhouses to hide away the filth that walks the streets of London. There is an unspoken connection between criminality and legitimate society as it is society itself that makes those on the poverty line criminals by class distinction, and in turn, those see no other option in surviving only to turn to criminal acts as they are seen as way from the beginning just because they are unclean, unfed and have no money, no purpose in life and are a burden on the society that London wants to convey. So why not take what you want as you are already classed a criminal?

Human Desire through Milton's Paradise Lost

By Ashling Mcgee

From the beginning, God gave humans command over the world, including nature and animals, but God also gave humans the responsibility of maintaining the earth. Humans started taking advantage of the land, taking more than they needed to obtain what they most desired. Did the fall from the Garden of Eden make humans fall away from nature? In this essay, humans are the main focus, especially their desires and what they will do to gain more; also, how Satan, painted as the devil and tempter, has a human side hidden away by sin and revenge. Throughout Paradise Lost, humans are supposed to be in control and not be tempted to stray for their desires, but they do, which causes harm to nature and the earth they are supposed to protect. In Milton's Paradise Lost, humans are doomed after the great fall from grace, as they commit a sin and their hearts are changed. God created humans to be in his image and likeness. God created Adam and Eve, bringing them to this Garden of Eden to develop and maintain a world for him. Using plants and animals is not based on domination but more as assistance.

In parts of his book, Milton places the blame for the destruction of natural harmony on humans' intervention in the natural world. This we see as Eve plucks the fruit from the tree: "Forth reaching to the fruit, she plucked, she ate; Earth felt the wound and Nature from her seat Sighing through all her Works gave signs of woe, That all was lost" (Milton Book ix, 781-784). This refers to taking the fruit from the Tree of Knowledge, which was not allowed. It inflicts pain on the earth, and Nature responds by unleashing a process of misery, withdrawing from the perfection it once held. This tree felt sorrow and pain as Eve had taken more than she needed, dishonouring the connection between humans and nature. When Eve did this, it broke a link that connected them to heart; hence, there was no working together in harmony as trust was lost between them. She even further violates the tree by giving Adam a piece of fruit. Nature responds more intensely: "Earth trembled from her entrails, as again In pangs, and Nature gave a second groan, Sky, lowered and muttering, Thunder, some sad drops wept at completing of the mortal sin (Milton, book ix, 1000-03). This makes nature angrier and deeply saddened at how Eve could abuse nature's gifts not once but twice. Nature weeps as a thunderstorm erupts in the sky as a response to its destruction of the earth by humankind. This shows that the least little act that goes against nature changes the balance between humans and nature with lasting effects on nature. It shows us how the effects of a small sin can grow and destroy something beautiful, such as picking a piece of fruit from the

Tree of Knowledge, and how unbalanced it links humans and nature. These ripple effects trickle and grow bigger as humans disobey the order of things. The violation of the Tree of Knowledge represents both good and evil, but choosing the side that destroys the earth and all that lives there has lasting consequences. Milton shows that all of God's creations have free will to choose whether or not they wish to serve him. "Sufficient to have stood, though free to fall" (Milton Book iii, 99). Everyone can stand tall and courageous but also be vulnerable to fall and destruction. Before the fall of humankind, Adam and Eve served as protectors of this earth, only taking what they needed to sustain themselves and labouring or attending to nature to maintain its beauty and survival. This temptation to want more knowledge, not knowing precisely what that was, caused the fall of humankind and earth's protector. Something was taken from the tree beside the fruit. This was a symbolic notion as it was humanity that was taken. This great fall that Milton talks about is the separation from nature

and humans existing as one. Adam and Eve are forced out of

Eden to an uncertain future. This is a lesson from God. They

have to repent for their sins. They can be forgiven if they

acknowledge what they have done and re-root nature to

show forgiveness for what they have caused.

In Paradise Lost, Satan is a fallen angel looking for

revenge. He cannot overpower the human will, but his lies

and desires can corrupt and tempt them, not forcing them but

making their own free choice to choose evil as it promises

more knowledge. God has placed them in this environment

to grow, learn, and create with their freedom while

respecting nature as nature provides them with this life. God

willing allows them to judge for themselves, and it is their

choice if they wish to turn away and disrespect nature, but in

doing this, they create a rift between human and spirit, which

has long-lasting effects for both sides. One can be

judgemental when we look at Satan's character as a fallen

angel who wanted revenge. He created an army to exact revenge on God and the angels, but he also showed signs of humanity as he had nostalgic feelings for heaven, asking if he could not be just content in God's presence and not disobey and sin. Is Satan right when he suggests it is better to reign in Hell than serve in Heaven? Would it be better to chase after the evils that exist to win instead of turning what is bad into something good and pure, working together with nature as one and creating the best possible outcome for humankind and nature.?

When Satan comes to Eden to tempt Eve, he is disguised as a serpent sneaking along. Humans would do this to disguise themselves instead of showing their true selves or hiding their true persona. So Satan in Paradise Lost is humanised as serpent-like, so many humans hide behind a mask in disguise. As Satan is a tempter tempting Eve to do evil, it may be motivated by revenge or envy of Adam and Eve. This jealousy makes him very ugly and shows his human side, as his envy and desire show us that Satan, even in his disguise as a serpent, has human failings.

Satan waits for Eve to be alone and knows that she is inferior to Adam and would be easily tempted by his charm. Satan could have feelings of lust or want towards Eve as she is beautiful and would want her as she may remind him of his former mistress, Sin. He knows that tempting Eve will "dishonour" her (book ix, 297). He tempts her by flattering her beauty, calling Eve "Queen of this Universe" (book ix, 684). This gives Eve confidence and a feeling of worth as she is beautiful and can rule the earth how she wants. It is God holding you back from moving forward. Satan tells her he has eaten the fruit from a beautiful tree and gained reason and knowledge. "Ye shall not die: How should ye? By the fruit? It gives you life, To knowledge" (book ix 685-687). Satan tells her God cannot hurt her as it gives her life. God is greedy; he wants you to stay and not learn more knowledge, keeping you from learning new things.

Believing in Satan, Eve takes the fruit and destroys humanity and nature. It is like a wolf wrapped in sheep's clothing. You think by the way it tempts you with its actions and words. Every human has fallen at some stage with temptation as it lives in us all, even Adam and Eve. It is one's own choice in what to do, which is why it is called free will, but some feel restrained by this, thinking they are not free to choose. This is where Eve felt trapped, not having free will as she was inferior to Adam and bound to him, but she fell under the temptation of Satan, and she tempted Adam to eat the fruit. Was she like Satan? That is why he felt drawn to her as he saw something similar in her that was like him. When Satan enters the Garden of Eden and sees Adam and Eve happy, enjoying each other's company and the animals playing around them. Satan falls into a self-pity state. Why can't he have this? What is wrong? They should not be allowed to be happy if I am not. " To you whom I could pity thus forlorn, Though I unpitied" (Book IV 374 -375). Self-pity is a human trait that shows us Satan has forms of humanity. Milton's portrayal of Satan is humanised through actions and his turning into different animals, which can reveal characteristics of humanity like the serpent, which to humans represents slyness and being sneaky and deceitful. It connects the creation of humans and animals and how we all wear disguises to hide behind. It shows our connection between humans and nature and how we break that link to achieve something better for ourselves without taking responsibility for the harm we are doing to nature.

It is free to attain the highest goodness or the lowest evil. Earth is of great importance as it provides life and water. Earth is like our mother, who provides food, shelter, and clothes for its children. Have we, humans living on this planet, given anything back to it? When the earth was created, it was filled with beauty, marvellous trees, colour, scent and wonder. This forest was a home for all animals and birds. The rivers ran through the mountains within this forest. The water was so clear you could see right to the bottom. The planet was pure and clean. With humankind's creation, the earth we now live in is getting destroyed by us as we are the disease-spreading evil enslaving Mother Earth, tearing away at the precious gift she bestowed us freely with her heart. It now weeps at what we have done in disrespecting her and not maintaining it the way we should be. Take deforestation, humans due to greed and capitalism transformed the beautiful forests that once graced the planet into bigger cities, urban uses and even colonisation of land to have more and more power and success. Green forests are being replaced by ugly concrete ones that we do not need more of. Deforestation is mostly in tropical rainforests. The forests there maintain a balance in the atmosphere and provide enough rainfall to the world. However, this balance is disrupted by human destruction, causing some regions to have excess rainfall while others suffer drought. The land there is also damaged, and replanting an ecosystem is complex. If we do not stop this, it will destroy all the rainforests. Humans are flawed, but it does not mean we have to accept these flaws in our world. Each of us is given a choice to turn a negative into a positive. Evil and good both co inside together. One cannot live without the other. This is shown through love and hate and peace and war. You must decide what part you want to participate in as a human being. Human activities are why global warming is increasing at a fast rate. Each year, our summers are getting hotter and hotter. Earth's temperature is rising twice what it was 50 years ago. Humans are causing this by air pollution, causing a rift in the ozone layer as an increase in C02 gases goes excessively over. This leads to melting ice in polar regions and increasing water levels. Humans are causing this by dumping chemical waste into the water, destroying the life in the water. Plastic has been thrown into the seas. Marine animals are affected as they consume it, and their health deteriorates. Oil spillages destroy the ocean. This is down to human greed being influenced by power and money, not caring about what it is doing to the earth and the destruction humans are leaving behind.

"Human nature is like water. It takes the shape of its container."(Wallace Stevens). This shows us that we are like liquid substances that can be placed or influenced inside a container controlled by its master. To do with as he pleases. Take hunting as an example. These animals are hunted and forced inside a trap and killed for sport. Animals like elephants are killed for their tusks; even animals with horns are smuggled in from other places after being hunted and slaughtered just so a person can display horns on its wall for pure greed and pride. Humans can stop this, but do not continue it for sport and fun. Animals like this are now becoming endangered soon; none will be left. The earth was created for all living things, not just humans, to control and take what they wanted. They were given life to maintain what was already there as the land and nature provided what was needed to survive. Humans became greedy and wanted more power, as shown in Paradise Lost as Eve was tempted to eat what was not allowed to gain more knowledge that she did not need as she had everything she needed to survive but wanted more. Greed took hold, and that is how the balance between humans and nature was lost as the connection was broken. This has to change. Our planet will burn out, and nothing will be left to save. We must work together, human and soul, to balance each other out to survive. Humans are the problem or disease causing the rift between nature and humankind. It is their greed and desires that are destroying the earth's core. Mother Earth is crying out in pain, and we, as humans, are not noticing what we are doing. We are starting to wake up but have left it too late. We must repent and re-root the balance between nature and humans again. We are the foreigners on this planet and have destroyed what once was a luscious-filled forest of beauty, animals, scents and clear-flowing rivers that once lived on this planet. One needs to wake up, begin to take notice of our surroundings, and listen to one call out in pain and cry for help. It is the daily things we do and take for granted that what we need to start with and little changes will help, but maybe, as humans, we have left it too late. We let our desires take over and forgot what Mother Nature gave us, and we disrespected her. She is fighting back with everything she has, as we have destroyed her. Now, she will destroy us unless we change and give back the balance and work as one with nature the way it was supposed to be from the beginning.

<u>History Lens</u>

This Lens gives insight into history from different aspects and eras, such as the French Revolution, women's history, Irish history, and history from Europe and worldwide. It can open the eyes to the past, its relevance in today's society, and what it might hold for the future of the next generation. We all learn from the past, which helps us see the present-day society and how it has changed or stayed the same. It could help us know what changes must be made for the future and to better our society and world. It is up to the reader to ask questions about life and whether our past conflicts with our present. Are people changing their ideas or sticking with the traditions of what they have been taught? Is the world changing for the better or the worse? Has the past and present contributed to how life and nature are now?

<u>Sublime Through The French Revolution</u>

<u>By Ashling Mcgee</u>

One must address the word 'Sublime' and its relationship to terror. This can come in objects where one is terror, and the other is seen as sublime. The sublime's beauty expresses intense anxiety when thinking of the French Revolution. Hence, the sublime is not just an embellishment in the exaggerated language of the revolution itself. When you see the slogan that portrays the French Revolution, "Equality, Liberty, Fraternity", was embedded in many works of literature such as Burkes, Shelley, Dickens, and many more, which explored ideas of human existence on earth and the liberty of the human mind, profoundly influencing romanticism and the sublime of the French Revolution. Burke sees the Revolution in terms of wonder and horror but not with complete blindness to what was happening. In Reflections On The Revolution in France, " In viewing this monstrous tragi-comic scene, the most opposite passions necessarily succeed and sometimes mix in mind; Alternate contempt and indignation; alternate laughter and tears; alternate scorn and horror" (Burke 10). Burke shows us how sublime and terror mix and change within the mind and how sublime can be reversed into terror. Compare this to Dickens 'Tale of Two Cities' which was written well after the event itself as his opening line ", It was the best of times it was the worst of times, it was the age of wisdom, it was the age of foolishness, it was the epoch of belief, it was the epoch incredulity, it was the season of light, it was the season of darkness…."(Dickens, 7). These writers show how sublime and terror can be displayed as a spectacle and theatrical event. They have an embellished style of sublime to grotesque, and how it exterminates the difference between them.

Burke establishes both the sublime and the beautiful as self-preservation and society. He uses self-preservation as the passion of weakness and society as the feelings, such as intimacy and communication. He sees those gaining power from their institutions connecting with terror, which causes sublimity. His belief of the French Revolution as sublime, in one way, thinks political power is sublime and could damage one being. However, in another way, the violence of the opposition is also a form of power that is also sublime. They contest the power that threatens the order which protects society from unravelling. Burkes 'Reflections on the Revolution in France' is a theatrical text where Eighteen Century sublime and gothic fictional conventions tell reasonably ordinary horror tales. He describes females as beautiful, males as sublime, women as familiar, and men as reserved. Burke proclaims that all will say beautiful is associated with emotions of love and affection, which we tend to compare with motherly figures. Kings and fathers are sublime masculine figures as they produce social passion of respect as they are feared, and one should submit to them. Burke wanted to join this idea of the sublime to a divine level. He saw terror as sublime through the horror and violence in the French Revolution on an earthly level. His concept of God is sublime as he viewed God as the object that brings power and morality together. This Godly figure is beyond a man's ability to make sense of him. The man keeps going to gain significant power as high as God himself. However, when reaching the summit, their imagination decreases as climbing up and up, and they are now afraid of the sublimity of its power. Burke has the idea that power is sublime, but it is also the form that is terror. He insists on the superiority of imaginative power with acts of God and thoughts of punishment and pain.

The eighteenth century was linked with the sublime and terror, and those writing about it used the sublime to fill it with terror, but some chose to clear out the terror. However, the combination of terror and the sublime carried great peril to the imagination. Dickens's writing of the Revolution portrays some of the events during the era, like the storming of the Bastille and the use of the Guillotine, a horrid machine used to behead the victims. Using history and fiction, he blends them when he recreates them in his novel 'Tale of Two Cities'. He expresses the antithesis of idealism and terror during the revolution. Dickens's characters were essential to him, and the names he bestowed on them had great significance. He used characters to represent the terror and the sublime in his novel. Like Carton and Darnay, his characters are linked to history's accurate and imaginary figures. Dickens uses two cities, London and Paris. One is terror, and the other is a haven. He describes Paris as a place of fearful enchantment where streets are violent, bloody, defensive, and unclean. The imbalance of how Dickens sees Paris and how it bothered him greatly. The one he knows is a place of light, fantasy, and pleasure, but not the one he describes. This city of light and destruction gives two images of sublime and terror. The readers can see this through the character Carton, who gives his life to the guillotine to save his love. Carton was brought through the Paris streets on his way to die, which shows that the city had this enchanter working for the Creator. Carton will die, but Paris will be set free, seeing Paris as beautiful again and its people's resurrection of freedom from the violent past. Dickens captures a story filled with historical darkness, but hope prevails, giving sublime during the terror surrounding it.

Shelley brings the sublime further than Burke, as Burke brings an understanding of the sublime in scrutinising the spectator's attitudes. The sublime shifts to a dream-like power in the observer, and the sublime structure is not unmanageable by the imagination. Shelley approaches the sublime by the very nature of the mind and filling up any spaces left open. He locates power in places where sights and sounds are visible and within the mind. Shelley uses violence in his 'Masque of Anarchy' that one would call terror. He calls it Anarchy. He tries to demolish political violence when speaking to those victimised. Using sounds of nature to emphasise blood and violence as "Till as clouds grow on the blast, Like tower-crown'd giants striding past, And glare with lightning as they fly, And speak in thunder to the sky" (Shelley 29). He uses images of revolt violence, turning it upside down. Shelley's image of people will disobey as they have no fear. The terror is insignificant to them. Looking at these different approaches to sublime and terror, you can see how sublime has perplexed reason and imagination that transcends and ignores all structures of meaningful delineation. Burke's use of fear and terror did influence others as it strove to narrate terrified emotions more dramatically. The involvement of objects and conditions such as darkness provoked Burke's sublime. Dickens captured the sublime through the mixed responses to human despair. Shelley's sublime was connected to nature with its sights and sounds to emphasise blood and violence. All very different approaches still show that terror and the sublime are connected, and one can interlink with the other.

Women's History through Radio Podcasts – By Ashling McGee

What can we learn from radio podcasts, and what can they tell us about our history? It is a new way of learning about insightful history from the past and today's society. Patricia Baker, who works in arts and media and is one of the founders of Curious Broadcasts, is a passionate storyteller who brings to life real women's stories and how these women played a vital role in Irish history and shaped it for the new generations. Baker also brings to light issues that were happening in the past but are continuing in today's society. It is great to see that in today's society, women are now a focus in Irish history and how they contributed to shaping Ireland from the past to the present day. Listening

to documentaries focuses on the mind as you have to

imagine what it was like and pay attention to the words

spoken. Listening to the documentaries like 'The

Troublesome Nun', 'Egg Money' and 'Do Disturb' by

Patricia Baker opens your mind. It gives you a sense of the

reality of Ireland in the past and Ireland today, showing us

how women were obsolete or never considered part of Irish

history back then. It opens Irish minds to what we dismiss

or push away as we do not see what is in front of us and

what is happening right under our noses.

Patricia Baker narrates 'The Troublesome Nun' to

reveal the revitalised role of individual women that

changed Irish society. Baker's documentary tells the life

and work of Margaret MacCurtain, who sought to teach a

generation to think about the past of women's lives. She

also devoted her life to writing women into today's history.

Patricia tells us of a remarkable woman in history. Baker, a woman in her fifties, looks at the next generation and how women in history are now a focal point in today's learning, unlike back in the past when women were rarely heard of. Women who were never heard of are now talked about by a generation eager to learn about women and the critical roles these women played throughout Irish history. This could not be done without women like MacCurtain. She lived in a turbulent century and was a woman who shaped how women were written into Irish history. She challenged and voiced her opinion on getting things done with women's rights and how they were viewed throughout history. She worked alongside the new generation of students and their vision and knew that the way of learning about women in history needed to be changed.

A woman on a mission, MacCurtain wanted to wake the public and the academic world about women's history. In Nineteen Eighty-Seven, MacCurtain got women's history courses on the curriculum in U.C.D.

Listening to the documentary, you hear from other great women who speak about MacCurtain with great pride. They tell how she influenced them throughout their life, like the former president Mary Robinson, who talked about her with such affection and honour, and how she encouraged and influenced her in her position as a woman and becoming a leader. The documentary tells of one woman's extraordinary courage and determination and how her outspokenness influenced the new generation of women to Stand proud and fight for their place within Irish history and society. The podcast showed how women of strength could change how future generations teach and view women's history. MacCurtain's love of life was infectious, impacting so many whose work and courage for women not to be seen as invisible and disregarded.

Listening to 'Egg Money' by Patricia Baker was insightful. It told about women in rural Ireland who were dismissed and seen as nothing but homemakers and had nothing to do with their contribution to improving life in

the Irish countryside. These women were just seen as

mothers and homemakers, nothing more. This documentary

tells us of women who are now in their seventies and

nineties and the lives they led in the past. These rural

women were working women with farms and houses to run,

and they did it without question as it was to be done.

Everyone helped from an early age. The cows were milked

before school, which was done by hand back then. Working

the land was not just a man's work. The documentary tells

of the hardship women faced back then, teaching the next

generation of women in today's society that women did

work, not just by doing the housework. It was a hard life in

rural Ireland as you had no electricity, so you had to light

an open fire for tea and food to be cooked and kept lit for

everything to be done. Patricia talks of one woman, Mamo

McDonald, who was a reborn feminist. She did not start to

be one but became one. She campaigned for women's

rights, including social, healthcare, and financial

independence. The documentary emphasises how women

were undervalued.

Previously, women had to give up their jobs once

they married. Even partaking in sporting events was not

seen as fitting for a woman as it was a man's game.

McDonald's involvement in women's activism began when

she joined the ICA group (Irish Countrywomen's

Association). Joining this group was the start of learning

new crafts and meeting other women. Still, it soon gave

McDonald a voice where her opinion counted, and she

helped bring about rural families gaining access to

electricity and piped water into their homes. Baker sheds

light again on how women brought about change through

their activism with women like Mamo McDonald and many

more who have not been recognised until later in life for

their contributions to Irish history.

The documentary 'Do Disturb' is a piece that hits at the heart. It is an eye-opener to today's terms of slavery and human trafficking. Baker hits hard with this piece, and as one listens, one thinks about Ireland and Human Trafficking. She opens with 'Slavery, a word steeped in history'. This makes one think of the history of slavery, and in today's society, it may have changed names, but it is still present today.

J P Sullivian talks of Human Trafficking that they are people who walk beside us daily. They could work alongside you, a person you know but do not see them. The world has not changed throughout history with Fedrick Douglass's speech in 1845 as an enslaved person. It has been altered with a new name but with the same agenda. It is a recurring nightmare for so many. The impact of COVID-19 is that the people, as modern-day enslaved people, are not sinking further into a black hole with no way out. Baker tells of an Irish Charity, MECPATHS, which is working with hotel groups to give programmes on how to see and the protocol of reporting sex trafficking. Hotels are places where many women and children are sex trafficked. The documentary is a way of spreading public awareness as Ireland is falling short on how big an issue it is—giving the Irish listeners a wake-up call to all the victims who are pushed down this dark hole and forgotten about. She aims to wake the Irish up and notice what is happening in each town and village across Ireland. Kevin Hyland, an anti-Slavery commissioner who is fighting against modern slavery and Human Trafficking, says that the amount of Human Trafficking that is going on in Ireland is unreal and to listen to the reports of numbers is shocking and disheartening that it is happening in Ireland and as a nation we let it happen either by ignoring the problem, or we are unaware as they are no public awareness of what is happening. One judge's immigrants and Human Trafficking are the same but have different identities. That is where the public is confused about how Human Trafficking goes unnoticed and keeps happening. Baker is voicing public awareness for Irish people to sit up and pay attention to what is happening under our noses.

Baker highlights reality not just in the Irish past but in the present. Her broadcasts are filled with stories and give facts about Irish women who changed the course of Irish History and how women were a significant part of shaping Ireland today. Baker shines a light on what is happening here and now regarding sexual exploitation and how, as a nation, we need to do something to stop this from happening, as it is a recurring cycle. She combines the past and the present in a way that makes a person sit up, take notice, and think about the world we live in and the world we want our children to live in.

Gender Relations throughout Early Modern Europe
By Ashling McGee

Gender relations within Early Modern Europe showed that in the Sixteenth Century, women's status was based on factors such as gender and social identity. Women were noted as inferior people within society. Even at young ages, girls were trained throughout Europe with lessons in domestic skills. These lessons were to bring them up in a society where these skills led to marriage and creating a home life. On the other hand, boys were taught skills about their fathers' station in life, a tradition of skills that the boys carried on. They did receive some schooling like reading and writing, which girls were not a part of. Marriage was perceived as both sexes' most critical aspect of social adulthood. Different countries in Early Modern Europe had other ideas regarding marriage and spousal relations. The insight into gender relations in Early Modern Europe sheds light on how women were seen between the 15th and 16th Centuries. Women were perceived as homemakers and reproduction vessels with little or no power or choice within the society they lived in. Both the Church and State of male rulers dominated society. Women were inferior, and men had 'Priority' as they were God's first creation.

"Wives were to obey their husbands, true to them and in some ways fear them" This was according to the Law code of the territory of Salzburg, Austria, from 1526. The male is seen as God's ruler as they feel they have this honour bestowed on them as a creation of God. Women were made from a bone belonging to Adam (God's first creation) as they were an afterthought and only made to service the male. In Polish society, women and marriage were set around the superiority of the husband and the wife's acceptance and submission to his authority. Women could not think for themselves as that was what their husbands were there for to tell them what to do. They did not question their husband's authority by having their ideas. This reflects to the Church and God that relations between a married couple were like those between the Church and Christ. The Church answers to Christ and is God's subject. This was the way for women, their husbands' subjects, to answer without scepticism. Husbands were to love and respect their wives like Christ was with the Church. In some ways, from the 16th to the 18th Century, marriage was, in some small part, a partnership in most European countries. Women had limited access to social sectors and were confined within specific control areas. When selling property, anything financial or legally binding, a wife could not do this without her husband's consent. A husband could dispose of property and sign legal documents by signing his wife's signature. Holdsworth says, "Marriage is a gift of the Wife's chattels to her Husband".

Women who married no longer had any power or rights regarding contracts like making a will, the property she had before marriage; nothing could be done without her husband's permission. Regarding inheritance claims, this was a complex situation regarding local traditions. In 16th

Century Portugal, it was considered that the oldest male sibling inherited almost everything. It varied what the girls could inherit with laws which gave parents control over their children, especially on sexual and marital conduct regarding their daughter. A girl was disinherited if she had relations with a male outside the marriage union or if they got married without her parent's consent. For instance, in Austria, all children are equal in inheritance claims; whether you are male or female, the property is divided equally. In Poland, a daughter would only inherit one-quarter of the property, and a son would inherit the rest. By the mid-16th Century, a law called Chelmno Law was to cause outrage among Gentry. The law was to have equal distribution of property between heirs regardless of sex. It also stipulated that "Conjugal community property with rights of the remaining spouse to half of the deceased's property". This did not sit well as the Gentry opposed it all at the Prussian directories, stating they wanted their daughters only to have a dowery of movable possessions, whereas their sons got everything. A widow can only use the estate after her husband dies; she is never entitled to own it. After a husband's death, a widow gets some economic freedom, but it is also restrained by the fact that women lose their principal source of income. Women who worked were subjected to community and trade restrictions even if they had worked with their husbands in a trade position. After his death, they were met with harsh conditions, especially regarding wages, given that they received less than they should have.

It was seen that women were to remain at home as housewives and tend to duties such as household chores and caring for the children. Women who did work were by a patriarchal system, which discouraged them from advancing economically, just like the division between male and female labour, which made it difficult for women to succeed. The housekeeper and bailiff were masters and mistresses who controlled a noble household. Although they had similar duties within the household, the bailiff was still superior as housekeepers were described as "Womenfolk's work". Marriage for the Swedish Crown greatly influenced his people as he looked for men with bailiff skills, and the wife came as a bargain, an extra labourer for less money. A man's status in life was linked with his work or social standing in society. A woman's title was only connected by her marital status and bond to a man. Regarding church patriarchy, it was an all-male-gendered society in which choices in certain areas constrained women. A woman bound by marriage had to honour her husband by obedience; in the eyes of the church, women were their husband's subjects. In early modern Europe, the parents decided regarding children's future, especially the girls, which was never questioned as, at a young age, they were taught the virtues of obedience and surrendering to male authority. These patriarchal societies made women inferior and fearful to speak out against it in fear of the consequences that would be inflicted upon them

as a result.

<u>Vagrancy in Ireland in 1822-23</u>

<u>By Ashling McGee</u>

The Poor Law Inquiry in Eighteen Thirty-Five was an investigation of poverty in Ireland that was written and published by the British government. In this investigation, those exposed to circumstances such as Vagrancy or those who may have witnessed this type of circumstance are invited to give evidence about the elements of their lives regarding Vagrancy. Vagrancy, which is the focus of this essay, shows that the number of vagrants is variable depending on the plenty or sacristy of provisions: it was much increased during the severe summers of Eighteen

Twenty-Two and Eighteen Thirty-One. Choosing this particular section to focus on gives us an insight into Vagrants and how they struggled through difficult times. It makes people aware of how they can fall on hard times and what they must do to survive. The inquiry was limited to the discussion of seven subjects; one of these subjects is Vagrancy, which is the one area on which I base my essay. The inquiry tells us different aspects of the lives of Vagrants and how it impacted their daily lives. The essay will discuss five areas: family relationships, food, work, begging, and shelter. These will show how it impacted Vagrant lives and the telling of these through the Poor Law Inquiry.

It was difficult on families and family life; relationships were affected within the family unit and as individuals. One area in which families differ is between town and country family life. In towns where the whole family begged for food, the family members separated, which divided the family unity. They may have gotten more from separating as individuals as towns would be clustered with people begging in dire situations. Vagrants' relationships within the family unit were affected in different ways, and in Conamara, men, women, and children travelled seven miles from their homes to obtain work. The men would receive seven pence for whatever work was given to them, and the women and children would only get half that amount for carrying baskets of sand and gravel where the horses could not have them. (Kelly) Women and children worked as hard as men but received much lower wages. The masses are industrious labourers, tradespeople, and proud people, but when poverty touches them, they must beg. (Mullin) The children of beggars turn out to be industrious and respectable members of society. (Corbat). Those who are proud and do beg only do so until, hopefully, work comes again, showing their children that even in the harshest of times of poverty, you can still become a respectable member of society and not abuse the kindness of those who help you as some might. A man lodged in a house supporting himself entirely by alms complained of back pain when asked to work for a decent wage. "I told him that I thought to stand up straight and labour would be better than stooping under a load of potatoes".(White). Some became complacent about the generosity of others, while others strived to keep their pride and work for their place within society. A woman with a family to support and who could not walk far would get a stone and a half or two stone of potatoes a day. However, a non-disabled man would get much more than he could consume. (White). Women and children suffered a great deal during these harsh times. In Tuam, there were small cases where older people would transfer their property to their children, and they adapted to a vagrant mode of life for the rest of their days. This occurred only with children who treated their parents with neglect. This shows how family relationships could have been fractured as older people turned to a vagrant way of life, a better situation than not being looked after by their children. This was only in minor cases, but the family dynamics were still broken. Mr Large says, "In town, though the whole family be begging, the members of it generally apply separately. In the country, I believe they mostly travel together. This gives us an insight into how families differ in town and country and the family dynamics.

In country areas, the family mostly travelled together as a unit. There were mostly potatoes, and cabbage was also given. Mr Collins says they are given potatoes with meal broth and broken meat at mealtimes at the shopkeepers' and gentlemen's houses. The town did have more to offer regarding food. The labourers in a town area were more liable to be reduced to beggary than country labourers. In the country, labourers might have a small piece of land that could supply them with a few months' consumption of potatoes, which would help if they were out of employment. The town labourers had nothing, so when work failed them, they immediately turned to beggaries. During the season of potato digging, vagrants were well supplied, getting more than they could consume each day. Some travelling vagrants would go selling prayers and, in turn, sell them for money to buy alcohol. On such an occasion, it was described that a woman lodged with a family who went out selling prayers. She returned with a bag of potatoes to sell to the family, but they would not have the money till the next day. She asked if they could take the potatoes on trust and give the money the next day. " I then said that though she was living on charity, she did not have a spark of it herself. She would give no trust. This shows that a person living on charity herself had none in return to give. (Michael White). Instead of helping, she buys whiskey and is selfish. An imposter who preaches the word of God and, in return, does nothing to help. She was greedy, and, in some ways, vagrancy has turned those into hardened people who have lost their fate and used it to their means. They have lost their dignity and soul and turn to alcohol as an aid or a crutch to lean on. Not all are like this, but it does happen as you have hit rock bottom, can find no way out, and do not care about anyone but yourself.

Vagrancy is more common in the summer and autumn as food is scarce. The males within the family leave in search of work overseas or to a country district for work after having sowed their plot of land, perhaps half a rod. Women and children close the cabin and turn vagrant. This was a way of surviving for most as, coming towards the summer, only some provisions were left after paying unreasonably high rents to landowners. Mostly, the female class turns vagrant. Some non-disabled men beg as no work is available and are generally ashamed to ask for money or food. The relief of beggars falls on the middle classes, such as shopkeepers, small farmers, and even labourers. The wealthy class is almost exempt from this as their doors are closed where the doors of the shopkeepers are open. The class difference shows us that it is the poor who support people experiencing poverty, as one day, they could be in the same situation and feel for those who are stricken with poverty. A man having as little as one stone of potatoes would give to someone in distress. Vagrant relief does not fall on any one class. It is shown that farmers and shopkeepers encourage vagrant beggars. The upper class feel it is a duty to discriminate against a person. A person owning half an acre of land gives more food unless they are beggars. Begging is seen as a trade, and charity as a duty custom induces many to give. Relief may be extorted in towns by insistency, but this does not occur in the country among farmers. As a charity, the Irish are governed by the feeling of St Paul 'thinking no evil', so they give food to vagrants whose characters are ignorant. Farmers prefer giving food to money as, for many, that is what they have at hand. Within the community, the poor give in larger quantities than the wealthy. It is people experiencing poverty who support people experiencing poverty. People experiencing poverty are there to help, as the gentry are generally never there. Diseases in the country seldom spread by giving them night lodging, some carrying blankets, and others having nothing. There are non-disabled men among them who are willing to work and ask their neighbours if there is any work to be had rather than beg. They would be willing to work for their lodgings or food.

Vagrancy advanced gradually over ten years but rapidly over five of those years. This can be due to the lack of improvements within town areas. It was mostly in summer that you would encounter an influx of beggars, as in winter, there was government work, although they were not much better off as they received no payment for the job done. This, in turn, increases the number of vagrants each year, getting bigger and bigger as non-payments and no work available. The only alternative was to live on the street and beg for some food. Some carried spades with them, wandering the roads and knocking on doors, where they might walk for miles, searching for any work available. They would work anywhere and do anything to earn food for themselves and their families. With the increase in taxation and the decline of the linen trade, those weavers became labourers, and every trade sank in decline. The decline of the linen trade was severe, as every class that lived in that industry was injured. Those who have lived in a time of vagrancy returned to the industry as soon as the cause that drove them was removed. Although the Poor Law Inquire was not politically successful, it provided a social resource for historians. Seeing how people experiencing poverty struggled and managed to survive gives us an insight into eyewitness accounts of the living conditions in Eighteen Thirty-Five. As we can see, there was a difference between the vagrants in the town and country areas. There were disadvantages and some advantages for those vagrants in the town and the country. This was regarding food supply and sheltered areas. Within the charity, it was primarily people experiencing poverty supporting people experiencing poverty, as those in the gentry class were absent from their estates. The higher class were obliged to give charity with some discriminations attached. Some have done it regarding the notion of rewards and punishments from Christ as "what you give, you shall receive back"—to some, vagrancy increased partly due to the great famines that triumphed in Ireland, which ruined so many lives. It also weakened others into habits of vagrancy from which they have not recovered. In some cases, pride took hold; they were ashamed or felt shame. They would not apply for an application even though They desperately needed relief. McNally said, "The children told me they had lived for two days on a meal of potatoes. This they suffered rather than beg at length; the mother and five children turned out and went to a strange place to pray while the father remained home. It is hard to see any one person suffering, but the children, it is hard as they are defenceless and need great care and attention. Pride is a big issue as it stops some from looking for help. It is the children who suffer the most

from the pride of the father as he feels ashamed that he can

not provide for his family, and it is a downfall as those who

suffer are the most at risk of dying, with the likes of children

suffering needlessly at the cost of pride.

Developments from the 19th Century shaped Ireland into today's society

By Ashling McGee

Ireland underwent a process of 'Modernisation' in economic, political and social ways. This is contested as what distinguished the country in the mid-twentieth century was inflexibly pre-modern. It is interesting how different layers of rewritten historical events that happened many years ago remain unique in Irish minds and lead to a belief in liberation. The Great Famine was central to the making of modern Ireland. Social changes, which began well before 1845, the Famine helped mould already surviving historical groups, giving them a new meaning. Post Famine outlined different directions for the North and South of Ireland. This included aspects of political, religious, economic and cultural identities. The partition in 1921 saw the North of Ireland with a Protestant majority. Thus, the remaining part of the United Kingdom, the south of Ireland, became an independent state called the Republic of Ireland. The Famine and the barrier greatly impacted the population of Ireland. Concerning events like the Great Famine, which significantly impacted Ireland, how Ireland's history shaped the economy, society, politics and religion can be seen.

One effect the famine had on Ireland was emigration. Irish emigrated to America during the famine times and after the famine years. It gave the United States the resources needed to help its economy expand, and the Irish grew to be an accepted element of the American melting pot. Nineteenth-century Ireland had a unique population history. The most populated growth was in rural areas. It then began to fall as the famine came, and farming was unsustainable. The famine divided the attachment of the rural Irish to their native land. Opportunities opened up elsewhere, giving way to emigration. In the later part of the nineteenth century, the push towards emigration had to do with the evolving nature of the rural economy. The flow of information from abroad created rising anticipations, thus distorting social life within

Ireland's countryside, making it unattractive for younger people to live in. Those who did emigrate came back but only to visit as they had undergone a social change, making it difficult to settle in rural Ireland. Famine gave way to the start of a new, profound life within a new country. It shaped Ireland today as those who ventured from Ireland helped build America's economy. Industrial companies would not be possible in Ireland as those who emigrated to Ireland and helped build up American companies have brought these companies to Ireland, giving opportunities to Irish workers. Would this have been possible without emigration and building America's economy?

It could be said that famine in the nineteenth century surfaced somewhat a new rule of governance committed to tactical interventions and social and political reform. There was a significant change in the Irish land structure from an indigenous system based on the rundale scheme; now, it was based on the new ideology of 'scientific' farming and agricultural modernisation. The Irish consolidation of land gave way to a shift from tillage farming to pastoral agriculture. At the end of the nineteenth century, land used for potatoes and grain was halved, making way for livestock rearing exported to industrial areas in Britain. The view of Irish agriculture shows Ireland's rural society as similar to backwardness, poverty and exploitation. Small farms were inadequately run, and it was no match for England's agricultural revolution with its increasing mechanisation, land management and breeding of stock. Ireland and farming remained under-capitalised, and those who worked made a living from tiny plots of land. Farming became more about rearing beef cattle and sheep by more extensive methods and moving away from labour-demanding tillage. These agricultural changes gave more freedom for the younger generation to focus on other jobs and futures and not have to work the land like their ancestors did.

Ireland's nineteenth-century religious transformation was a devotional revolution. According to Larkin, "the great mass of the Irish people became practising Catholics" in the nineteenth century. After the traumatic famine event in history, the loss of the Catholic language and the shattering way of life for Catholics caused a reaction to an identity crisis. Catholics were now ready for a sculptural revival. Paul Cullen, Archbishop of Armagh, reformed the Irish church and, in the process, led the consolidation of a devotional revolution. Irish people became practising Catholics and have remained still to the present day at home and abroad. With change comes responsibility, and the first synod of Thurles, which took place in 1850, was the first government of the church by bishops since 1642. Cullen created this; he made it so the church would be reformed from the top down, and the bishops would be responsible for enforcing the reform. This was difficult as many bishops disagreed with reform. The bishops had educational and political differences, inhibiting their efforts to reform the pastoral system. Cullen was an influential clerical politician. He had the support of Rome, especially in church appointments. "He reformed the Irish church in his generation". Cullen promoted men like Kilduff, who were men like himself. They were good preachers, courageous and young, and had no personal ties or loyalties that could inhibit their devotion to reform. Cullen accomplished a complex and subtle combination, ignoring the trafficking of nationalist politics based unfeasibly on his interaction with Rome. The priest's political role was mainly accepted by the people, showing a sign of the confessional nature of life in Ireland. The papal cause in eighteen fifty - nine till eighteen sixty showed the commitment of Catholics in Ireland as an Irish Brigade of Saint Patrick went to the papal state to fight for the pope. This tells us that Irish Catholicism, like Cullen, was driven into a political attitude. Organised Catholic politics was developed, and the difference between

Anglicans and Presbyterians in Ulster seemed less critical. The spiritual passion of the eighteen fifties and Catholic snobbishness in the same decade reinforced their common Protestantism. Politics plays a significant part in today's society. The separation between the North and South still plays a vital role in how church and state orders are made, and the constant battle in peace negotiations from long ago is still carried out today. New governments that come and go with new ideas still cannot seem to agree on their religious differences and lay them to rest.

In the late nineteenth century, Mary O'Brien Fogarty, daughter of a Limerick farmer, spoke of her childhood memories. Mary Fogarty's family adopted the church's focus on civility, modelling themselves on the Protestant elite, adopting Victorian hierarchical values and new respectability ideas. The family went to mass in their plain chapel, said the rosary every night, and dismissed the belief in fairies and other customs as peasant superstitions. Those who worked for the family practised different belief systems. A servant called Dooley remained stern in her beliefs, defending the fairies as Dooley and Mary argued over the credibility of fairies as Mary attempted to convert Dooley to a more orthodox Catholicism, saying fairies were "wicked Sassenachs". The memories of Fogarty's family show that post-famine Ireland still upheld various religious beliefs, exposing different types of spirituality and rituals in many communities. In a time when Cullen tried to confine religious practice to the chapel, everyday parishioners demanded a religion that echoed their traditions and customs and interacted with the supernatural. In the early twentieth century, when Christian synodal legislation was passed, it slowly altered how people experienced their parish rituals. Mass, confessions, and marriage began to move into the church slowly.

One aspect that nineteenth-century Ireland helped shape today's society was beer production. In some ways, it may be seen in a lighter context, overshadowed by more significant events like the Great Famine, the Land War, and religious divides. However, the economy produced barley, still the most excellent beer in Ireland today. Even Irish abroad still look for a feeling from back home, and there is no better way to have it than a pint of Guinness. At the end of the nineteenth century, Guinness became one of the largest breweries in Ireland. In the Great Famine, government relief measures were introduced into rural Ireland, the economy was confined to the eastern seaboard, and money spread through a depopulated Ireland. Guinness sales rose quickly until eighteen sixty. The main factor was that the brewery's expansion no longer belonged to the English market, but now it was a growing part of the Irish rural market. The consequences of the famine were pivotal for the brewery industry. Throughout the famine, the sale of beer rose, showing evidence that the beer market did not lie with the people outside the maritime economy. Commercial brewing in Ireland experienced growth in 1790. This transformation was due to the Irish parliament legislation favouring the development of brewing instead of distilling. Parliament members believed beer drinking benefited the working classes and the Irish economy more. Irish beer exports to Britain from the 1820s were that Irish brewers enjoyed lower raw material costs than English rivals. Barley was cheaper in Ireland as agricultural labourers' wages were lower. The construction of Irish railway networks improved rural market access for urban breweries. Larger Irish brewers exploited the opportunity presented by railway networks to expand into rural markets. The construction of Irish railway networks in the mid-nineteenth century allowed Guinness to build a great trade in rural Ireland. In areas where peasant culture survived well into the present century, the porter had become the popular drink on the western seaboard. Guinness acquired a reputation for its healing qualities as it was the whiskey and poteen before the famine. Guinness advanced with their beer through the famine, exploiting the railway system to their advantage. They are still a significant part of Ireland and its history and evolving in many ways.

The famine did help people profit from it. Lessons were harsh, but the Irish were rooted in their old prejudices and old ways that nobody could induce them to make the changes the famine brought about in their habits of life and agriculture. Catholic Ireland continued to be a multi-layered, diverse island. It was significant in economic and social change, religious transformation and regional variation. Irish and Catholic have become interchangeable terms in Ireland—even the attempts of nationalists to make Irish rather than Catholic the inclusive term did not work. Father Tom Burke put it very well by saying, "Take an Irishman wherever he is found, all over the earth, and any casual observer will at once conclude, Oh: he is an Irishman. He is a Catholic. The two go together". Even now, no matter where you are, Irish and Catholic, you are not one without the other.

It could be fair to say that economic conditions improved from 1840 to 1900. However, the culture of poverty was broken during the famine and determined by continuing emigration, leaving the remaining population less poor. By the twentieth century, the relationship between Ireland and Irish communities worldwide had become symbolic. Emigration during the famine helped advance Ireland locally and abroad, benefiting America and Ireland. It decreased the island's overpopulation and helped America with its economic growth. This, in turn, helped shape Ireland today.

Rushdie's 'Midnight's Children' The Human Relations Through Life of India

By Ashling McGee

Literature is not restricted to one part of human life, as many aspects of humankind exist. In some of Rushdie's writings of "Midnight's Children," hidden issues must be revealed. He conveys his points regarding politics, culture, economics, and history, which are not central or straightforward and revolve around his main subject character, Saleem. His story is exciting and sometimes light in that the reader is not overwhelmed by all the significant events in India during that Pacific period. Rushdie is somewhat critical of the communist movement, although sympathetic toward some communist representatives. The communists are seen as illusionists, but the people hold on to reality undivided. Saleem describes Picture Singh, a communist leader, as an antirepublican but also stated, "I can say with utter certainty that Picture Singh was the greatest man I ever met".

Midnights Children's novel tells of a particular imagination of Indian nationhood. It exquisitely allegorised the partition of India, creating a commentary that addresses its reality. Rushdie describes Kashmir as a reflection of past and present, as Saleem himself describes Kashmir through Aadam history. Saleem cannot return to this place as it has changed, and the Kashmir he talks about does not exist anymore. It once was like a paradise that lost an area of tranquillity, but the struggle between India and Pakistan has destroyed that picturesque view of what it once was.

Rushdie uses two allegorical imaginations, personified in the novel Midnights Children. These two figures are Saleem and Shiva, who have different ways of thinking and acting but were born simultaneously as the nation of a free India. Saleem is a Muslim, and Shiva is a Hindu, both different religions with different outlooks. They are like yin and yang, which have been linked together since birth. The use of Nose and Knees is relevant within the story. Saleem's nose represents his telepathic abilities as it is believed to read not only the emotions of those around him but also gives him the power to communicate telepathically with other children born simultaneously. Shiva's knees bring all his opponents to kneel before him—with all their ideas and histories, fighting and arguing like political representatives. At the novel's start, Kashmir is forgotten or left to one side, beginning the book not with the birth of India but with Saleem and Shiva's birth. Did Rushdie do this on purpose so as not to take away from his real story, which was Saleem and his journey, or get bogged down in too much historical context and overload them with it and taking away from his main subjects, Saleem and Shiva, the protagonist and the antagonist?

Nineteen Forty-Seven was a year of great importance. India became independent from the British Empire. Hundreds and thousands of Sikhs, Muslims and Hindus were subjected to horrific torture and death. Many left, not knowing if their homes lay in India or Pakistan territory. The partition questioned whether Nehru's vision of a new India would survive. Three decades passed, and nothing could relieve any fears and more bloodshed. The birth of Saleem portrays Midnights Children on midnight August 15th, 1947, the very same time British India won its independence from the British and was split into two new states that would rule themselves. These states became known as India and Pakistan, marking a significant time in history that Rushdie displays in his novel: "On the stroke of midnight, as a matter of fact, clock hands, joined palms in respectful greetings as I came. Oh, spell it out, at precise instant India's arrival at Independence I tumbled forth…"(Rushdie 3). The first-person narration is Saleem's voice; we are reading his story. It is a mix of imagination and actual events that are happening simultaneously. The significance is the clock and timing representing Saleem's birth and the birth of a new India. Saleem and India are now tied together in history. Saleem himself places himself in the present but is rooted in the past. Nationalism was fundamental in India for its struggle to gain independence from the British, unifying the masses for a common purpose. This unified identity was complex for Indians because of the various languages, cultures and religions. British India was divided along religious lines, forming the Muslim nation of Pakistan and the Hindu nation of India. India continues to separate itself further based on language and class.

Saleem is a Muslim, whereas Shiva is a Hindu named after the God of Destruction. Rushdie represents two opposite sides, which use private partition against public partition (New India). This is shown through Saleem's grandfather, Aadam Aziz, and how he falls in love with Naseem Ghani, a wealthy landlord. Adam is a doctor who visits Naseem whenever she complains of an illness. He crosses the lake to their house and falls in love with fragments of her as a sheet covers her each time. "Aadam Aziz's visits to the bedroom with the shaft of sunlight …

became weekly events… he was vouchsafed a glimpse, through the mutilated sheet, of a different seven-inch circle of the young woman's body" (Rushdie 25). He sees glimpses of her and not the whole person. He falls in love, and they get married, but it is doomed to fail as Aadam Aziz has abandoned his Muslim faith. In contrast, Naseem is very religious and becomes known as the reverend Mother who rules the house and family like a tyrant. Naseem represents Bharat – Mata which is mother India. Aadam made the mistake of loving only the fragments of her, which he could see and understand in pieces but not the whole piece as one, so they are incompatible. The story of Aadam and Naseem is, in some ways, a representation of Kashmir as the boatman Tai is the link connecting the present to the past, with the people with their customs and each other. He ferries across to and from the land of the ancestral dead. Tai is the image of an old man "plying this same boat standing in the same position across the Dal and Nageen lakes… forever." (

Rushdie 10). Tai tells Aadam, I have seen Emperors die, Muslim conquerors perhaps longing for Kashmir Emperor Jehangir. "what were the emperor dying words – I tell you it was Kashmir?". (Rushdie 14). Tai, a Muslim, does not represent only one religion or political system. He is timeless. Tradition can feel external, although it is not that; this is why Tai is shown as one to forego religion and Empire. Aadam Aziz is portrayed in Midnight's Children as the beginning of modernity in Kashmir. Aadam lost his religious beliefs as his time in Germany estranged him from Kashmir and its traditions. When he returns from Germany, modernity is fading, and traditions and practical identity, the unselfconscious practice of innocence, are lost or pushed out of the way. These are then replaced by a modern irrevocable affirmation of categorical identity – nationalism. Kashmir was like Eden Nehru said. Kashmir was a mixed but harmonised culture, accepted by all religions with no communal feeling of a definite identity. This can be seen within the novel by Tai's view of Kashmir as he sees it as a land to which Jesus turned after the events recounted in the Christian Bible. The novel Aadam is about Kashmir, although only a fraction of the people is represented by Aadam. Not all Kashmiris were connected with the outside world and were becoming modern. Look at Aadam and Naseem, for instance, and the Rowlatt act and how it was a mistake to pass it. The Act authorised the British government to arrest anybody suspected of terrorist activities. The police could search a place without notice and permission. Naseem wails, "What Rowlatt… this is nonsense where I am concerned"(Rushdie 37). Aziz thinks back on Tai and how it is said that the Kashmiris were different. Cowards, as if you place a weapon in a Kashmiri hand, they would never pull the trigger. Aziz "does not feel Indian, Kashmir, after all, is not strictly speaking a part of the Empire, but an independent princely state" (Rushdie 38). Naseem criticises Aziz because his ideas and enthusiasm oppose coming out of purdah.

Aadam tells his wife, "Forget about being a good Kashmir girl. Start thinking about being a modern Indian woman" (Rushdie 39), showing us that Naeem follows traditional communal ways and is a modern woman who breaks tradition and asserts a nationalised identity. Aadam is conforming to a more nationalised way of thinking.

In Rushdie's Midnight Children, one can see a novel that intertwines fiction with realism. His characters each portray a specific part wrapped in history. Saleem and Shiva are both "Victor and Victim" and have different upbringings. Their viewpoints work together as they portray optimism and pessimism. Saleem was reared in a rich environment, and Shiva was brought up poor and had a horrible home life. Two different social class backgrounds give them a different aspect of India. While Saleem's ego grew, Shiva's anger grew also. Shiva had a horrible life after Vanita's death. His father turned bitter to the point where he tried to smash Shiva's knees with a hammer, but Shiva broke his father's wrists between his knees. Shiva needed to be a fighter and become an influential military leader. Shiva and Saleem became rivals and wanted to take charge of the Midnight's Children conference – a meeting of mental voices through Saleem's telepathy. As they grow up, the other midnight children get divided, and tensions rise as world views of prejudice take over their minds. However, Saleem, born in a world of possibilities, hopes they will overcome and unite these views. Shiva laughs at Saleem's romantic views as Saleem believes anything is possible. Shiva states that no third option is available; there is just money and poverty, and there are haves and have-nots left and right. Shiva believes people with money can only afford to dream, whereas the rest have to fight. Saleem, wanting to have that attention, shuts Shiva out of the conference, and after Saleem finds out the truth about him and Shiva being switched at birth, he hides this as he does not want Shiva to claim his birthright and take all the attention away from him. This becomes

Saleem's downfall as Saleem does not become the traditional hero in the novel, as it shows his downfall. It is Shiva who becomes a war hero. Rushdie exposes the idea of the nationalist nation as a myth implying hope to be found with a new generation of Indian people in the hopes of generating a counter myth of their country. Shiva becomes refined and sophisticated and a great ladies' man and seducer. His affairs lead to children, and he leaves them as soon as they bear children. Saleem brings up Shavi's son with Parvati as he does not want to damage her reputation. The interlink connection between Saleem and Shavi now has this child who has both attributes, so maybe he is the one who will change Rushdie's novel. It was a combination of history steeped in a fictional tale told by Saleem, and it was his story to tell. Magical and realism brought us together, teaching us parts of history while guiding us on paranormal fiction. Regarding Kashmir and partition, Rushdie displayed it well in his book, hidden within the context of Saleem's storytelling. His story of his grandfather and his wife Naseem makes partitions, not just about different religions or cultures. However, he portrays well how different people and their differences cannot be suited to each other but remain married.

George Orwell's essay 'Shooting an Elephant'

By Ashling McGee

George Orwell's" Shooting an Elephant" (1936) is set when the British colonised Burma. Working as a British Officer was hated by many people. Young and ill-educated, he was afraid to speak out for what he really believed was the right thing to do. I have been part of a system with no escape. He is stuck between hatred for the Empire which he serves and rage against those who make his job impossible. An incident gives an insight into the nature of imperialism and the white tyrant's dominion in the East. It shows how an elephant becomes a victim of imperialism, and the officer is the white man who becomes a tyrant, losing all sense of morality. Knowing that it was morally wrong to shoot the elephant, the tyrant in him took over so as not to feel like a fool in front of the Burmese people. He shoots an incident animal to do his job for the empire rather than what was morally right. Knowing this makes him part of the system of imperialism and the elephant an innocent victim.

An elephant in this part of the world is a symbol of strength and power, but in this case, it falls victim to imperialism; its power and strength have been taken away. "he trumpeted, for the first and only time, and then down he came". This happened because a British officer does what a white tyrant working for the empire does instead of doing what is morally right. The elephant was not wild but tame, broke free from its chains, and escaped. The one person who could have perhaps saved the elephant was its owner, who had taken the wrong direction and was now far from the elephant. It was left to the British officer, now the only one with a rifle, to determine the elephant's fate. "they had seen the rifle and were all shooting excitedly". Being the white coloniser, the one with the gun, these people expected him to uphold his position within the British empire to shoot the elephant. "made me vaguely uneasy". This is where his conflict of mortality shows he was faced with the expectations of his position and, as a person, did not want to shoot an elephant. A white man in a position of power must not be frightened. The thought that if anything went wrong, those Burmese people who were watching me would see me chased, trampled on, reduced to the corpse and laughed at like the Indian up the hill. There was no choice in what had to be done: loading the gun and taking aim. With the first shot, all I could hear was the gleeful roar of the people. The elephant "neither stirred nor fell, but every line of his body had altered". This elephant was doing nothing, not even noticing the gathered crowd. The animal seemed calm, waiting for someone like his owner to get him. Instead, this poor elephant had now been shot by an officer who, instead of doing what he felt was the right thing to do, did what he was expected to do as a white coloniser. This shows imperialism taking over and an innocent animal facing the consequences. He did what he was there to do as an officer but as a person who, as we see in the story, has somewhat of a hatred for the position he is in, like when he says, "All I knew was that I was stuck between my hatred of the empire

I served and my rage against the evil- spirited little beasts

who tried to make my job impossible". He is stuck in an

awkward situation in this town, to uphold the law as a British

officer and the Burmese people who may hate him as he is

English but still expect him to do the job he is there to do

and protect them.

A British officer standing before an elephant who seemed

peaceful and did not mind anybody was defenceless against

the rifle he held aimed at the animal. He was watched so

intensely from behind by the crowd that had gathered of

Burmese people. "for it is the condition of his rule that he

shall spend his life in trying to impress the "natives" and so

in every crisis he has got to do what the "natives" expect of

him". I see this as a man doing what is expected of him as

an officer of the British empire but not as a man with a mind

or a heart of his own; obeying the rules justifies him in

killing the elephant, but as a person, it makes him morally

wrong. Feeling justified by his actions, the other officers it was divided; the older officers agreed with him; the younger officers thought that killing an elephant for killing a coolie (unskilled labourer) was wrong and that the elephant's life was worth more than a coolie. Ultimately, it all comes down to opinions and what some may think is right or wrong. In this case, the reason behind the elephant's killing is mistaken as he says, "I often wondered whether any of the others grasped that I had done it solely to avoid looking a fool". This tells me that he did it not because it was the right thing to do but because he did it to save face and not look stupid, making him more of a man for doing what was expected of him and not what should have been done. The loss of a beautiful symbol of strength and power fell victim to imperialism because the white man had the rifle and had the power and authority of the British empire to use it.

<u>Poetry</u>

<u>And</u>

<u>Photo Lens</u>

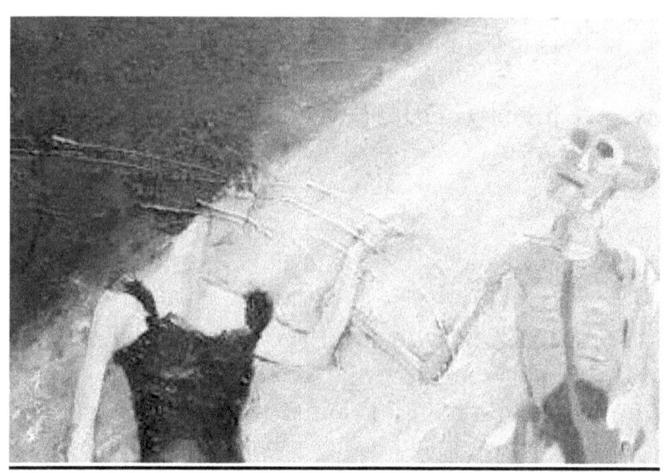

This Lens is seen through poetry and photos. Poems can tell a great deal, no matter whether they are short or long. They can evoke feelings and emotions and give insight into what happened when the poet wrote the poem. You can get immersed in a poem from the words written on the page, taking you to that time and place and opening your mind to what is happening then and now. A photo can also tell a story of a time and place of great importance and make you feel a part of that time and see what is happening in a different world than the one you live in today. Everyone has their perspective on how they see or read, and it is impressive that every opinion is different and unique.

Imagination and Memory of Life through Whitman and Silko

By Ashling McGee

Starting with the quote, "Sometimes what we call 'imagination' and 'memory' are not so easily distinguished" (Leslie Marmon). The relationship between imagination and memory plays a vital role in the works of Walt Whitman and Leslie Silko. Leslie's work is about storytelling and preserving one's history by retelling stories of the past from generation to generation, which reflects the present and future along with the past. Her work combines stories, poems, and photographs, which opens the reader's imagination as she writes her words, telling of the history and how storytelling is a way of survival for the Laguna people. On the other hand, you have Whitman, a mystic and a unique man, in his work. He uses imagery through his words to show his imaginative power in capturing the reader's attention. Even his self-portrait is unique and stands out to the readers. Both profound writers tell a great deal and, when explored, open a whole new world to the reader.

Whitman shows his impressions of the world, which reflect the present. His words make the past jump off the page, giving the reader a world view of what the future could hold for them. Although natural and vibrant, Whitman's images explore a world of memories. The images are represented as fragments of a dream of the world surrounding us. It is a picture of the life cycle, how one person communes with nature, and how humans are part of the earth's life. "Yet behold, it has room for all the shows of the world, all memories! (Walt Whitman – My Picture Gallery). The mind can hold so much and holds everything that a person sees, learns, and hears from a generation of stories told, as well as the presence of a personal life experience. This poem, 'My Picture Gallery,' is set in a small room where all these images on the wall surround Whitman. He may not remember them all, but they represent a memory that is important to him. (Figure 4). This connects with Leslie Silko's 'Storyteller', where memories are held and told to each generation to say to one's history and bring it into the present life. Exposed stories are often fictional and based on true accounts the storyteller has lived or heard about. It is a swapping of stories from gossip that one might have heard from the town or village of people talking, or some are from family stories passed down from generation to generation. Although some may be elaborated on or pieces added to it. It still represents one's history and memory from the past.

Figure 1 – 'Aunt Susie at Marmon Ranch', Lee. H. Marmon, Laguna, 1949

This image shows a picture of Aunt Susie and the workings of the land. She looks at a young child and shows different generations, stories, and memories of being there and learning about Aunt Susie's life. She passed down her wisdom and culture to the next generation. It is a memory in time and the retelling of a story about Aunt Susie and her life from the point of view of a child telling the story when they are grown up. "I remember only a small part., But this is what I remember" (Leslie et al., 'Storyteller', 6). The picture shows how memory can bring us back to a place and time and relive it by telling the stories you heard from a family who has long since passed away, but the stories remain in your mind, and the photo reflects these stories. It may be now more elaborated as you might have to fill in certain things you cannot remember, which is where the imagination comes from, making it more relatable and fictional for those to listen to this incredible story from the past. It is filled in how you believed it occurred or happened. Memory and imagination go hand in hand, and part of it may be fictional, but its memory is accurate, which is its most crucial part.

The truth is presented within stories, poems and photos of different versions one may read, see or hear. Everyone's life is a contact of culture haunted by past stories and memories. The stories, poems and photographs that are shared are subjected to the storyteller's past and their version of events. The reader sees part history and part fiction. These work together to form a piece that gives the reader a memory of something and the imagination of what it would be like if you were there yourself. Whitman has a unique personality. His work shares the mysticism of America, which at that time was transcendentalism. His work was near the end of this movement. His representation was one of assertiveness and independence. He was showing America as an embodiment of independence for many people. "Of every hue and trade and rank, of every caste and religion… A farmer, mechanic or artist… a gentleman, sailor, lover or quaker, a prisoner, fancy man, rowdy, lawyer, physician or priest" (Walt Whitman, 'Song of Myself', leaves of Grass, 33). His poem opens America to the world of possibilities that you are who you are and believe in yourself and the variety of human experiences. It represents the idea of self, relationship with the universe, and other selves. Whitman's

portrait naturally shows himself.

Figure 2. ('Walt Whitman as a young man, Gabriel Harrison

1854)

This picture or portrait was natural and honest. For an image

of that era to be taken in that form was shocking as photos

back then were more formal with dress codes, and a specific

style had to be portrayed. This portrait shows not just the author Whitman but also his poem 'Song of Myself', which represents the poem's image and subject—giving the reader both a memory and imagination a means to the world—looking at the world through a different lens a new pair of eyes to see things differently. The portrait rejects the norm because he stands casually looking, hand in pocket and hand on hip, as if this is me, with no expectations or high social standing. His shirt loosely opened on the top as if relaxed, not fixed for a portrait with a tie and button-up collar. He looked like an everyday working-class American. He was a wanderer in life, giving him a sense of freedom, and you imagine his travels as you travel with him and imagine the world with a new perspective.

The interlink between short stories and poems with photographs gives readers written memories, imagination, and visual images that one can relate to the subject. In Storyteller, Leslie uses the pictures her father took to give readers a feeling of the landscape and people in the Pueblo villages where the stories come from. The photos show a deep meaning and speak more than the written words of a remembered time. The story is not just words but is told through images. These images give the readers different emotions and respond in various ways. An image produces other purposes and can mean different things to readers. Her work is not just for entertaining the readers but is an identity which connects us all to the past, present and future.

Figure 3. ('Rain clouds and the Rainstorm', Lee. H. Marmon, Laguna Pueblo)

Looking at this picture, one can see this image as a beautiful landscape and nature, but it holds a more profound meaning to the Laguna people. It represents human survival. As the water was so scarce, these people depended on rainwater and these black clouds looming over the land brought a blessing as there would be water to survive. The poem that Leslie includes is more like a song, in fact 'The Go-wa-peu-zi Song' which is "of the clouds, and rain clouds, and growth of corn, I sing" (Leslie Silko, 'Storyteller', 48). This image and song fit together as the people sing for the rain to come, which is the memory of what the Laguna people did, and the image takes you to the place of dry land with dark clouds looming, expecting rain. Looking at the photo, a reader sees the nature of the land and sky as we see daily, which we take for granted sometimes. We expect our crops to grow, and we will be provided for no matter what. However, in this context, the land is essential for people to survive, and rainwater is needed. Leslie shows us how the Laguna people sing for the rain to persist; this is her story of how survival is essential based on nature. It opens the reader's mind to the fact that nature plays a vital role in our existence, and somehow, we seem to have lost that concept. This puts the present into focus and makes us realise how different lives and nature work for us. The past and present connect by imagining what it was like then and what the future may hold. Human survival reflects memories of today in the present.

Images expose aspects of history to tell us about past events, sharing visual memories that a person interprets differently. Their imagination begins to wonder what it would have been like back then if they were there or how it affects the future. Both Whitman and Silko give great insight into memories and imagination. Whitman was a man who stood out, making us readjust our values as a person and to nature and our relationship with ourselves. One of his quotes gives us insight into the kind of man he was, 'I wear my hat as I please, indoors and out'. This tells us of a man who rejected the norm of the society of that era, even in his portraits. You see him wearing his hat like in Figure 2, where he has it tilted to one side, giving him a sense of freedom or swagger as he does not care about society and how his appearance to others judges him for how he looks. His writing style was free verse, not constricted or conforming to the norm. He brought transcendentalism and realism into his work and is often known as the father of free verse. He used his writings to introduce readers to taboo topics of the human body and its functions, using unusual themes such as leaves, trees, and nature to combine humans And nature. Whitman's imaginative style united the reader as one, different but equal unity. In Storyteller, Leslie shared memories of storytelling passed from generation to generation. With these, she brought fiction and memory together, giving the reader an insight into the lives of the indigenous people and how storytelling kept their memories and presence alive. The images represent a look back to the people and landscape of how the Laguna people survived. It also showed how human survival depended on certain things, like in Figure 3, the rain clouds, which nature gave them the survival of crops and human survival. Her book tells of traditional tales she heard when she was young and included themes such as identity, tradition, and survival. The images she used brought personal feelings to each story she told.

Memory is represented in a narrative form through storytelling, poetry and photographs. History photography is linked with realism but creates an image with subjective choice. Photos tell a story on their own without any written words. How one sees these pictures and how one's imagination comes into context is personal. A memory means something different to everyone, like a picture from the past. It is open to interpretation. One can see how memory and imagination play a significant role in works like

Whitman and Silko. These two profound writers open our minds and let us explore their past and history. Giving us insights into them and the stories and subjects they write about. When readers begin to read a book, they are invited into a world unknown and subjected to different views and ways of life. Walt Whitman takes you on an adventure with each journey he takes. It feels as if you are experiencing it for yourself. He brings the world of America into a new light and a way one should live. His memories and imagination open possibilities of what the future could hold for you as a person, identifying with yourself and others around you with nature as its focus. He dives into subjects one should not talk about then and brings life forward with his openness and life experiences. He makes everything that is created divine. The world he lives in is the person who is strong, tranquil in mind, immortal and cannot be conquered. These people meet in fellowship, passing along the same roads worldwide. He brings everyone together under the same banner, where they are not excluded for who they are or what they have done in the past. "Neither a servant nor a master is I" (Whitman, 'Leaves of Grass', 69). It makes you think you are an individual, not a servant or a master to any. You are the master and servant of yourself. His work is still a great inspiration to others today. We see a man who defied the norm of society, stood tall and proud, and tried to get others to believe in themselves and look within themselves for who they are and what the future could be for them, even if it meant rejecting what society demanded of them. Silko was similar in how she told stories of the past and how the only way to keep them present and relevant was through storytelling and memories of the Laguna people's lives, how they communicated with themselves, and how they communicated with nature.

The memories shown through their stories, poems and pictures keep them alive and in the present that they matter and their lives matter and should be shared with the world. Silko uses her imagery to portray memories of her past and tells us a story that may be embellished a little as memory and imagination are combined to build an account for the reader, taking them on a journey along with actual events told to her as a child. Looking at the memory and using an image of how memory travels with us through time, even if some of our memories are missing, we still can look back and see them through pictures with pieces of memory never forgotten.

Figure 4. Walt Whitman, Samuel Murray, 1891

Whitman was surrounded by his pictures on his wall in a small room, sitting there and remembering his memories of where pieces were broken or missing. You can relive the experience and fill in the missing details with your imagination. He looked old and tired but still did not conform to a particular society, living in a small place surrounded by what he treasured most, the images of his life and those he held close to his heart.

Seeing Life Through Different Lenses
Ashling McGee

These are personal poems that give a self-perspective of life and feelings.

<u>Crying Out</u>

<u>By Ashling McGee</u>

As you walk in a hurry, can you not hear the cry,

Does anyone notice it fall and die?

It bends and twists as it reaches the top,

Would you even notice it as it slowly drops?

It bends its way down slowly, it falls,

Crying out in pain, nobody hears it call,

It suddenly snaps and falls with a thud,

Its mother sways, weeping, watching as it is covered in mud,

Vanishing out of sight beneath the ground,

Been walked over time and time still; nobody hears the
screeching sound,

Calling out in pain and weeping so loud,

Passing each day, if only one would look up from the
crowd,

Next time you go out, stop and look around,

Listen closely, and maybe you will hear the weeping sound

Always There

By Ashling McGee

As I lay thee down to sleep,

Do not be sad, and please do not weep,

I am at peace and up above,

Looking after you, all the ones I love,

I am with you everywhere and every day,

I do not plan to leave; I will always stay,

Although you cannot hear or touch me,

Just look to the night sky, and there I will be.

I will be the brightest star shining up there,

No other star in the sky will compare,

Know that I love you, and I am always around,

Even though my feet could not touch the ground.

Move forward with your life and reach for your dreams,

Each day, trust yourself. Life is not always as it seems,

Things can go wrong but always come out right,

Never be afraid to look up; I will be your guiding light.

Leaving Behind

By Ashling McGee

When I leave this world for the next,

I hope I have checked some items off my bucket list,

Everyone has one, no matter what they say,

We push it to the back of our minds and say, "We will do it someday,

I want to tick some off before that day arrives,

I want to achieve something in life and travel with my daughter to make memories that last,

Memories she holds dear to her heart once I have passed,

I would love to travel to Nashville and feel the country music flow,

Meet a genuine cowboy while at a Rodeo,

Then there are simple things like spending time with those you love,

When you leave this world, you can only watch from above,

When I am gone, I want all to laugh and cheer,

Fill your heart with joy, remember the fun times and hold
them near,

At the top of my list is the most important of all,

Carry on living; make memories; finish your list no matter
how big or small,

Bring me with you along for the ride,

I am always there with you, right by your side.

Breaking Free

By Ashling McGee

Standing there in the pouring rain,

It is striking cold, but I feel no pain,

It is running down my face, but I do not care,

Just standing here in total despair,

Let me out. I need to be,

Looking in the mirror, there is nothing to see,

Want to go where there is no pain or tears to cry,

Wanting to feel like the raindrops that come pouring down

from the sky,

Nobody knows where they will land or lay to rest,

Every tear cried every drop of rain is some test,

Every tear dropped may wither and die,

It is how you move forward that makes you survive.

Renewal and Rebirth through Sylvia Plath's poem The Elm

By Ashling McGee

Plath's poem The Elm is supposed to be about rebirth and renewal, but as it finishes, there is a hint of death and destruction. Plath gives the tree the voice of a female figure, which is spoken through the poet's mind. As a woman, the tree knows nature's truth through personal experience. She describes love and her loss after losing it with an agonising pain: the sunset and the destructive power of the moon pulling at her. "Love is a shadow" shows us that love is beyond hope, like a horse galloping away, and the only sound you hear is the horse's hooves. This Elm tree represents a connection between nature and humankind and how they are linked. In the poem, the tree is a mother-like figure that nurtures, and the tree's roots are the womb that runs deep within the earth's soil. Merchant links that the abuse of women and the environment are connected by documentation, ideologically and experimentally, in the historical development that she claims, 'The death of nature.

The Elm is a symbolic tree of the Tree of Wisdom/Knowledge in the Garden of Eden—a struggle between nature and humankind. Plath says, "So Murderous in its strangle of branches?" this can mean that hidden away between these branches is something dark and evil separate from the tree itself. Plath could be talking about herself that she is the darkness hidden there. Merchant believes that there are two core principles of ecofeminism, and both are the domination of women and nature, which are connected. Anthropocene could be seen as an ecologically tricky situation, an era of non-knowledge linked to uncertainties and supernatural unsettlement of human mastery and the domination of the earth's system. From the first stanza of Sylvia Plath's poem, her use of "I Know" twice tells us that she knows the tree's knowledge. Even "She says," tells us she refers to the tree as a female identity. The poem's reader may fear the inside, but the tree does not. Plath uses the Elm tree as a significant frontline focus in a controlled image, using its roots and far-reaching branches to uncover a vision that spans the day and the seasons. She uses images like 'The sea, ' representing distress, and 'The Moon, ' which is seen as this authority figure from outside looking down. Is it possible that nature and humankind are linked? Humans influence nature and know now that this power it holds over nature is becoming unstable and unmanageable. Plath's reference to 'The moon' is this pull towards it as if it is trying to pull the tree from the earth. The moon is seen as a dominant figure wanting to harm this vulnerable tree as it is now bare with no leaves for protection, but the tree catches it. Then it releases it, and it is necessary to do so—both fighting for a position within the planet. Val Plumwood shows us that human essence lies in expansion control over the natural sphere and qualities like freedom and superiority of the material sphere. Along with nature and humankind, the volume is caring, showing sympathy, and an understanding of the circumstances of others. Taking some responsibility for others is a signal of our virtuous being.

Throughout Plath's poem, we see the feminine influence as the tree and moon are feminine identities, but both struggle. She talks about love loss and the tree's roots as she feels the connection between humans and nature's feelings. As she describes it, love lost is like a horse that gallops away; the only thing left behind is the imprint of the horse's hooves. The connection between nature and women is the changing seasons, an image shown through the tree and how she suffers through each season. Even when she says, 'Wind of such violence', stating that this cruel wind whips at my skin as I fall apart. The harshness of the wind shows how she feels raw and in pain. Then she says, 'My red filaments burn and stand a hand of wires', showing us how love destroys you to the point of leaving you weak and having no energy to continue. The interlinks that Val Plumwood puts to us are alien and inferior, which are not worthy of respect or respectful knowledge where connections cannot be easily made. There are three problem parts. These are the formulation of the human, the formulation of the self and the formulation of nature, which connect again. Sylvia Plath's writing is centred around womanhood and nature. Merchant argues that there is a universal female behaviour and goes against the portrait that constantly casts women as nurturers. Women and nature have a long-standing relationship which has persisted throughout culture, history, and language. Merchant tells it that her analysis is not to let nature be the mother of humankind, nor should women become the role of nurture dictated by historical identity—both of these need to be set free from this stereotype label that surrounds it. Val Plumwood's idea of feminism was one of mistrust. It combined the romantic formulation of women and nature, the idea that women share this closeness towards nature that is unsharable to men. It seems to be the opposite of feminism as it gives a positive value to being barefoot and pregnant, an image of women and justifying their exclusion from a world of culture. A feature of ecological, feminist positions that gives positive principles to this connection between women and nature. However, in previous times, especially in the West, it was given a negative cultural value and was the main ground for women's subjection and degradation. Plath says, 'I am terrified by this dark thing, That sleeps in me' She is troubled by infertility as this process of childbearing is linked with pain, fear, and anxiety. She is afraid to be alone giving birth. In a male-dominated society, it is an essential value of womanhood that they reproduce just like the earth is fertile and produces. For those barren, whether it is women, land or animals, it was unforgivable and unacceptable. The Moon in the poem is jealous of the tree's ability to bear fruit when the moon is left barren, dragging the Elm Tree cruelly and not knowing who will win this constant struggle between them.

The poem shows images that clearly show the aftermath of destruction. Threats and hurts are felt within her poetry, both inside and outside the female body. Humankind is subjected to the sufferings caused by humanity, whereas the environment is vulnerable to toxic fumes, smoke and pollution. It is not the love lost that kills. The crack in a woman's mind destroys you from within. Women are like forests that have been destroyed and cleared of everything. Gender abuse is nostalgic for natural abuse. These both serve the male desires. Women's contribution to development is ignored. The state of womanhood appears unexpectedly from the communication of products that exterminate natural resources and social diversities. The poem explores a female voice and the response to a material and cultural system destroyed by pollution. 'Shall I bring you the sounds of poisons?' Not the taste, smell, or sound; it is the least used to identify the poison. Then the rain comes, and instead of cleansing it and the tree bearing luscious fruit, it does not 'bring forth in white like arsenic'. It could be seen that acid rain is falling from the sky, destroying nature and everything it brings forth. The Elm is returned to the Garden of Eden at the end of the poem with the snake hissing, representing the three parts: the formulation of human, the formulation of self and the formulation of nature connecting again. These three parts are combined, and we cannot survive without all three together. They struggle within themselves but must learn to co-exist in some shape or form. Just like the moon is jealous of the elm tree, but as the tree captures the moon, it must set it free.

Danez Smith's poem 'Dear White America' and racial injustice

By Ashling McGee

Danez Smith's poem 'Dear White America' relates to racial injustice and inequality in America. It states the violent abuse and death of many black lives and how it is not changing anytime soon. The sentiment of trust plays a significant role in Danez Smith's poem as one goes in search of a new God, as the one that has been given is untrustworthy. They are tired of white people not seeing past the colour of their skin. The title is a direct message to all whites to take notice and listen to what has been said. The mentioning of names highlights black people who have been killed as a result of brutality by the police and violence within the American system. Using only the first names given to them at birth brings the reader and listener closer to them as human beings and reminds them that they are people, no matter their skin colour and that their deaths are significant and mean something. Smith uses the word 'Bid' to express different meanings in his poem. 'Bid you well' expresses a wish, 'Bid you war' involves the expression of violence and 'Bid your own lives to gamble with no more' is the taking of black lives from this white world. This poem is a statement or a call for those to notice a broken system that has enabled brutality, difference and racism against those of colour. I have found two theorists that relate to this poem, Dorothy Roberts and Frank B. Wilderson III, who convey through Smith's poetry and his message that he is trying to get out.

Racism is a modern-day invention that exerts power and is not the product of race. Race is a system of control that labels humans into political ranking based on invented biological differentiation. Racism causes many health problems in those with coloured skin, resulting in social, economic and political oppression. Stress from racial trauma leads to changes in the body, destroying the physical well-being of black people. Racism is like cancer. It can spread quickly throughout the black community, physically and emotionally. Robert argues that 'Black' is identified as an enslaved person, whereas 'White' has a privileged property status. Another way to see it is that 'Whites' are superior and masters. ' Blacks' are inferior subjects or enslaved people to their master, who is white. Torture has played a role in which violence is needed to maintain white supremacy. Those categorised as enslaved people who would be black people are outside the ambit of humanity, giving authority to those within the humanity circle, which gives the white people unrestricted licence to inflict pain and brutality on black people. These are seen as subhuman and can be treated like animals and as the property of the whites. The system needs to be fixed as one chain of torture replaces another. As it developed from slavery, lynching and police whippings remain, as it is now the brutalisation of black suspects in the criminal justice system. In his poem, Smith talks about a new life where you cannot sell us, hang us, beat us, silence us or cover it up. He is talking about a history of abuse and brutality towards black people and that it keeps repeating itself repeatedly, and nothing changes. It is only shifting from one form of torture to another, and it has to stop. Those with white skin have to notice what is happening around them. They may feel safe and secure, but black people do not have that luxury. Producing biotechnologies endorses people's belief that race is a natural categorisation. Looking at a clinical trial, Roberts describes where they used only African American subjects for their practice on a new drug. This drug was intended to be distributed to everyone, regardless of race. The company then stated that it was only tested on black people, so the FDA should label it for BLACK USE ONLY. This is racism and shows that white is the standard of humanisation which black people are judged against. The drug is safe for all to use, but as it was not tested on white people, it is not deemed safe and should only be used for black people. It shows how whites are privileged and that drugs are acceptable only if white people are the test subjects. The drug was safe and could be used by all, but not by the whites ruling as they were in charge. This is similar to whites not having to fear every day for being stopped by the police for no reason, whereas a black person fears being pulled over and searched daily by a police force. Just because they are of a different colour, they are treated differently. This is conveyed in Smith's poem. He talks about the recklessness of the law and having to count his brothers in the morning to see if they are still there with him. It is about disrespect and being invisible, as whites control everything and everyone. Smith describes that at his brother's funeral, the white people make noise and do not respect the person's bones that are lying there beneath the soil. Why should they care? It is the norm for white people that black people disappear and are invisible to them. That is the way society sees black people of no consequence to them as they are living in this bubble of safety, and nothing can harm them as they have the power. This is similar to what Wilderson says about being a slave to its master.

Wilderson tells us that without master-slave dynamics, our fortified world would collapse. Black people will never be seen as human beings. Still, they will remain enslaved people tied to those who call themselves white masters. He talks of Afro-Pessimism, which shows a map of human experience where those of colour are fundamental in human society but are always at all times and in places. The framework for Afro-Pessimism does not consider black culture and the individuals of black people; it instead focuses on the production of knowledge and the consequences in political form. Wilderson used Hartman's theory that anti-blackness is contained in everyday areas other than significant moments of spectacular violence. Afro-pessimism views that black people are still equal to enslaved people. Like other Afropessimists, Wilderson believes different skin colours, like Asians, Latin Americans, etc., are small partners in a white society and are involved in a small degree of the profits of non-blackness. Those of black skin are the outcasts of society, considered enslaved people denied humanity, and exposed to violence. Even historical incidents like the civil rights movement have not changed the progress of African Americans in society. The violence that is set in motion and the position of the enslaved person is all-inclusive that the state of existence of social life is destroyed by the state of reality of social death. In social life, a person is a victim of violence if one disobeys the customs or orders into which one was born. At the same time, social death is a threat of violence that has no meaning whatsoever. This shows that a black person is open to violence on a whim of a civil society ruled by white people. A black or enslaved person has no access to their ancestors or their "conscious community of memory" (Patterson). Social death haunts black people as it has no meaning for it to have happened in the first place. Black people must be killed for civil society to live. This means that the whites want a culture of coherent white life and not an irrational black one. They want to suppress black people from being visible and stop them from being represented as real individuals as human beings, so they try to kill it by keeping black people invisible to give power to white civil society.

Smith's poem displays how black people are unfairly profiled and unequal. He says we did not build your 'White' prisons, yet we fill them all unequally. Locked away like animals for crimes we did not commit. Only black prisoners are confined in these cells as whites believe we are at risk in your white society to which we wish not to belong. People are colour-blind and refuse to accept that what is happening is wrong. These acts of brutality and violence are just expected of you and are deemed acceptable as the whites say it is. You unquestioningly accept what you believe is natural, but it is not. Take off the coloured glasses you wear and see what is happening around you. Race plays a part in what is happening to black people, but racism is the more significant issue, and accepting it as a natural society you live in. This has not changed throughout history, as black people are still regarded as enslaved and profiled into this category. Whites still act like the masters of black people, holding this power over them, using it and enforcing it to fit into society as a natural behaviour. Will this ever change, even with the changes made throughout history? It is still an issue and will always be if blacks are still profiled as enslaved people and whites act like masters over them.

<u>Milton's Paradise Lost – By Ashling McGee</u>

Milton's Paradise Lost Book 2 extract from lines 402 - 429

is a unique, detailed, and descriptive literature. It tells the

reader of Beelzebub's proposal to investigate this New World

of Man and turn it towards corruption, destroying God's

work of humankind. Accepting Beelzebub's bid by the other

fallen angels is attractive because now there is a need to find

a volunteer within the group to go on a journey to investigate

this new world. It causes tension and silence among all

gathered. Milton's use of blank verse allows him to delve

into detail with long, drawn-out sentences, using similes,

Oxymorons, and Onomatopoeia placed within this piece of

literature. This piece of writing is of dark, mysterious

literature. The reader gets a sense of silence as it falls upon

these warrior angels that one must volunteer for this lonely

voyage into the 'unbutton'd, infinite Abyss.' (Milton, 39).

Reading this work shows Beelzebub's manipulation as he

speaks to the other fallen angels, which is most interesting

as you discover a hidden depth within the extract and gives

dark mystical energy evolving within Milton's book. Milton

uses Beelzebub's speech to demoralise the other fallen

angels from volunteering, leaving one too proud to coward

away. It was an intentional act on Milton's behalf as he

wanted to portray Satan as a character of, a prideful non-

human entity. Satan is a complex character, in which Pride

is his most significant fault. The reader expects nothing less

from Satan but to volunteer himself. The theme shines

throughout Milton's writing, which shows the reader moral

choice, especially with 'Satan whom now transcendent glory raised.' (Milton, 39). The focus of this extract is on two characters, Beelzebub and Satan. Milton uses his writing to give the reader an insight into Satan, especially Beelzebub, through his wording and imagery. Milton gives off a dark, mysterious place, and hidden beneath is full of power and deception. All want to achieve power, but they are controlled by believing there is only one fit for this journey. In this extract, Satan becomes a hero as he alone can take the burden of this voyage even though it was done through manipulation by Beelzebub speaking on his behalf. He is giving him praise tactfully without arousing suspicion in the other fallen angels.

Lieb tells of a devotional reading demanded in Book 2, but is this how we are supposed to read Milton's work? (Lieb, 253). It can be heavy and bewildering to some readers. Some of Milton's poetic passages are excellently written, charming those who read his work. The extract can be portrayed as a devotional piece as it is like a religious sermon given by Beelzebub to the other fellow congregational members. They seek a volunteer to investigate humankind's new world and mould it into their thinking or beliefs. However, one could read Milton's work as a mystical, mysterious piece as someone about to embark on a dark, weird journey. Milton's imagery uniquely shows this: 'through the palpable obscure, his uncouth way, spread his aerie flight, upborne with indefatigable wings.' (Milton, 39). It gives the reader an image of a giant bird of prey soaring overhead, raising those tired wings with incredible strength—flying into the unknown Abyss. The reader's imagination opens as they enter a world where one sees this dark realm of mystery as one brave warrior sets on a voyage to brave this mystical darkness and search this world of humankind.

Wheeler points out how Milton manipulates the blank verse so that we cannot simply take the words, especially Beelzebub, at face value. (Wheeler, 368). Milton does represent the angels like detailed works of art. There is a need to pick away at the pieces to reveal the true face. The portrayal of Beelzebub as an unhuman figure contumelious towards God. His speech read with great conviction, showing a constitution of powerful speech that could manipulate others into believing what he said. He speaks, 'But first, whom shall we send in search of this world? Whom shall we find sufficient? (Milton 39). Milton's repetition gives Beelzebub direct force in asking who the bravest to take on this voyage. One could read that he is telling the others that there is only one worthy enough, and his name is Satan. Beelzebub may ask someone to volunteer but states that only one can do the job, so stay silent and not oppose him.

The manipulation of Beelzebub continues throughout his speech as Milton controls Beelzebub's characteristic narrative by speaking in a naturally controlling tone: 'Choice is our suffrage as the weight of all and last hope relies.'(Milton 39). Wheeler describes this as some memorable utterness delivered well in Paradise Lost. (Wheeler, 366). Milton's work shows this using words like 'Suffrage and Weight.' These, to a reader, can convey a political meaning, as if choosing the wrong figure to forge ahead on this voyage could severely cost them what they aim to achieve. Milton uses Beelzebub as a figure to make clear and direct his fellow members to think hard about the decision they are about to make and that there is only one possible solution: putting their trust in Satan. Agreeing with Wheeler, the reader can see how Milton wants to get his position of Beelzebub's character across as one can manipulate how the right choice is best for all and not oppose his decision.

Milton describes how the other fallen angels felt after Beelzebub had spoken; the reader could feel a deafening silence within as 'undertake the perilous attempt. All sat mute.' (Milton 39). Wilson argues that Beelzebub's performance is his devilish ability to merge and be blunt with the desires of the previous speakers. (Wilson, 14). It shows how Beelzebub is speaking for Satan, who needs someone to manipulate the other members into believing that he is the one that they should obey and choose him as their leader. The use of onomatopoeia here is placed very well within Milton's work as 'mute' gives the reader an imagined form of silence among all, not knowing what will happen or what the fallen angels will do. They all fall silent in the hope that Satan would volunteer so they would not have to. Beelzebub's and Satan's intention is to make them doubt themselves and look towards Satan to free them from this burden by volunteering himself. It is impressive how Milton uses one word to convey silence within a room of fallen angels trying to gain power. In a world of power struggle, Beelzebub dissolves this by merging the desires of the other speakers to conform to his way by following Satan.

Wilson does convey that destruction rather than construction is more appealing to the other speakers, and Beelzebub uses this to put Satan into a position of power. (Wilson 14). Interestingly, Milton uses a simile to get this point across in a political speech given by Beelzebub. After his speech, silence fell upon all: 'Satan now transcendent glory raised, Above his fellows with monarchal pride.' (Milton 40). This agrees with Wilson's point that it was a political strategy that Beelzebub used in his speech to convince those that destruction was better for all and that the one to lead them was Satan.

Rising with great Pride that he, as a ruler, would lead them towards glory. It was his time to prove his leadership. Milton's portrayal of Beelzebub is a mixture of confidence and manipulation as he is used to increasing Satan, a figure of great position, and making Satan more potent by using Beelzebub to praise him and make him more important as a leading figure to follow his command. Wilson makes an interesting point that 'Satan's consolidation of strength can come from sacrificing Beelzebub giving up his identity. (Wilson 14). It is evident to the reader that Beelzebub does not oppose Satan and volunteers for this voyage. He speaks of how he wants to mould this man's world towards destruction, yet he does not put himself forward for the journey to do this. It suggests a motive behind his speech, as if speaking on behalf of someone he deems more suitable or superior to him to take on this journey. It is present in Milton's work as 'His suspense awaiting who appeared to oppose or undertake' (Milton 39). The reader can see that Beelzebub is a pawn in Satan's game as he sat down and did not oppose or stand back up to volunteer his service for the voyage as if knowing it would be wrong to do so. It enhances the theme throughout Milton's work, which is a moral choice. Beelzebub chooses to sit down and be silent, believing it was the right decision, but was it? Could it be that Satan was the manipulator behind it all, using Beelzebub as a speaker to make all sit and believe that the moral choice they were making was the right one? Milton intertwined his words to give the reader a sense of deception and intention, which someone else manipulated. It could have been a political point in that sometimes, what we choose, we are not deciding for ourselves, influenced by someone into believing the choice we make is the right one for all involved. Milton gets the reader's mind to delve into something and manipulates them into thinking the right choice is what they say. It is taking power away from you to choose another way.

There are many ways to read Milton's Paradise Lost. One argues that Book 2 is more devotional, but some could read it as a magical, dark, mysterious setting wrapped in detailed artwork with layers beneath each section to unravel and search for the truth yourself. Milton uses his words in a style that gives a reader a sense of mystery and a feeling of complete silence, such that you hold your breath in anticipation of seeing what happens next. It can be hard to read, but once you open your eyes and delve into the detailed art form of the literature to reveal its true meaning, do not take the first reading at face value. Some have realised this, like Wheeler, as it convinces readers to look more in-depth at what is behind the painting, not its surface.

The reader can find pieces that show how Milton wants to convey his poetic form. Nafi states that Milton's words freely use myth and legend, and classical and biblical allusions are found throughout his writing. (Nafi, 21). It shows you can read Milton's work in many ways, not just as a devotional reading, Lieb states. Readers can choose to read it most compellingly and excitingly. It is conflicting in myth, legend, and religious terms. It has an air of mysterious intrigue that gives the reader insight into a dark, mystical place beyond our imagination. Milton beautifully portrayed this piece, and his language, style and imagery gave it such depth. The reader felt everything from the very start, and it opened the readers' minds and beliefs in myths and legends.

Milton's devotional references were detailed well without overpowering the readers' choice of how to read them themselves. The theme shone out through the book as a moral choice was a major significant factor, and reading it could persuade a person that those manipulating the situation were doing it for the right reason. However, if you delve further, you can see the manipulation of moral choice and make the reader think again about the decisions made in Milton's work. Using words like 'weight, suffrage, choice, and mute' made the extract even more enticing to the reader, giving them an image of darkness and mystical intrigue.

Photo analysis of Bill Hudson's photo of 'The Civil Rights Movement'

By Ashling McGee

Bill Hudson covered the Civil Rights movement in the 1960's with protests in Birmingham, Alabama, where police turned dogs and fire hoses on demonstrators.

Bill Husdon covered the civil Rights movement during the 1960s

Protests in Birminham Alabama led to Police using dogs and fire hoses on demonstraters

Birminham was one of the most segregated cities in the US and was notorious for police brutality

Birmingham was one of the most segregated cities in the USA, notorious for police brutality. The photo shows a police dog jumping at a teenager on May 3rd 1963, in Birmingham, which provoked outrage and put pressure on the federal government to act on behalf of Black Equality.

In Diane McWhorter's book 'Carry Me Home' she refers to

Bill Hudson's photo nine times, saying it helped move

'international opinion to the side of the civil rights

revolution. The image shows a white cop in dark shades

gripping a black youth and letting the dog attack him as if it

were just a regular occurrence.

The foreground features three main characters: the

teenager, the dog, and the white cop. This shows how

whites controlled the Black community in Birmingham.

Looking at the photo, he forcefully grabs the young teen on

the street, who is very passive, not showing any aggression

towards the cop. His eyes lowered with a non-resist feel.

The cop's sunglasses show that not having to look any

black people in the face as much as to say they are all the

same. What does it matter? There is no need to remove the

sunglasses. The youth's hand is on the cop's arm, but this is

to hold himself up as the dog viciously attacks the teen by

biting into the youth's stomach. The teen's face is one of

submissiveness, with no retaliation or anger. His arm is

down along his side as if in surrender, not even trying to

push the dog away from him.

Even if we see another white cop approaching him, holding

his dog back but still present to insert fear, it displays a

robust view of injustice and the struggle for civil rights that

is still happening in today's society. The background shows

onlookers but nobody getting involved. The black and

white print photo showing the clear presence of the white

cop would be the focal point that draws you in. The man in

the background looks back over his shoulder but walks

away in a different direction, non-confrontational,

submissive, and not wanting to get involved. The white cop

seems to exert power and knows he can without any

resistance from others in the picture shown as we see other

black people not getting involved. The dog being used is

just barbaric and does not need to be used to attack the teen

as the teen complies without any use of forceful means by

the dog. The white cop takes three focal areas: the black

teen and the dog. The white cop is the aggressor, the black

teen is the passivist, and the dog is the fear factor or

terrorise. It shows how the political science is evolving within the civil rights movement. The whites have control, and those of coloured skin are defenceless against it. The white cops use dogs as enforcers to assert fear among the black people who are helpless and submit to white dominance. The dog is used to attack innocent bystanders who are non-threatening towards their handler (The White cop), showing the violence between whites and those of colour and that whites are the most dominant.

 Photos can tell a story if you look at them and see what they are trying to say. Some give us great insight into history and specific movements that have a lasting effect. So, a picture can reveal more than one might suspect. It can open the eyes to a world that we may not see ourselves, but through the lens of someone else's camera, it can give us a whole story surrounding one snapshot taken in time. Remember, when you share a photo on any media platform, you are telling a story, whether it be about yourself or something entirely different. A picture speaks a thousand

words and tells a story and its true meaning.

<u>Conclusion</u>

As one can see, there are different forms in the way life can be seen. A world in which the past, present, and future can affect oneself can be intoxicating. Nobody has the right to judge, own, disrespect or even undermine another person. We are all humans and should be treated as one. This is not the life case, so self-care and mental state are essential to everyone. Nobody can take that away from you if you love yourself, no matter how hard they try. This is easier said than done, as with what you have read through the different lenses of how people are treated now and were in the past. They are similar, but this has to change, and everyone needs to respect everyone and everything around them. Nature provides, but often, we disrespect it and take it for granted, as some are greedy and want more when plenty is already available. With today's technology, it can be both discriminating and influential. How one uses these tools must look within and positively influence today's society and future generations.

The future generation will carry forward what you put out there. Nature and human life must be linked and work together to make a brighter and safer place for all. Open minds give us the tools to remake and mould the world for a better tomorrow. Through this book, great literature writers have given new light on a future that a person should strive to live in. It begins with loving the person you are and sharing that with others. Be yourself, stand for your beliefs, and never let anyone put you down and make you feel worthless. You are not. You have the power, strength, and ability to be the person you want to become and keep moving forward daily to be independent and love yourself and the nature surrounding you.

This is an old-age fight for self-empowerment. It is not something new; it is something forgotten and needs to be shared. Every human being needs to be treated as an individual and a person, not a thing or something valuable to another. Each of us is unique, and we all need to show it and be brave enough to live freely; that begins with loving

yourself and the nature surrounding you and never taking

any for granted. Love and nature are connected and should

be treated accordingly. Times may change throughout

history, but we can still submit or feel we must be put in the

right place. As one grows like nature, it flourishes and

thrives, but humankind has taken it for granted as everyone

wants more and more from it. This human error needs to be

fixed, and it starts with each individual loving themselves

for who they are and seeing the beauty in nature

surrounding them. We do not need more than we already

have, which is life itself. We learn from the past in the

present and try to make a better future for the next

generation to continue.

Seeing Life Through Different Lenses
Ashling McGee

Sources Used

Bibliography used in:

Sylvia Plath's "The Bell Jar" concerns a young woman's struggle for self-determination.

Badia Janet, *"The Bell Jar and other Prose"*, Cambridge University Press 2006

Baldwin . A. Kate, *"The Radical Imaginary of The Bell Jar"*, Novel Fall 2004

Bonds S Diane, *"The Separative Self in Sylvia Plath's The Bell Jar"*, Gordon and Breach Science Publishers, Women's Studies, Vol 18, pp 49-64, 1990

Martin Wagner Linda, *"The Bell Jar: A Novel of the Fifties"*, Twayne Publishers, New York 1992

Nelson Deborah, *"Plath History and Politics"*, Cambridge University Press 2006

Plath Sylvia, *"The Bell Jar"*, Faber and Faber Limited, 2013

12 Years A Slave – Book vs Film and the lens we see it through.

Berlin Ira, 'American Slavery History and Memory and Search for Social Justice, *The Journal of American History, Vol. 90, No. 4, Oxford University Press,* (Mar. 2004) pp 1251 – 1268

Cobb Nichole Jasmine, 'Directed by Himself: Steve McQueen's "12 Years a Slave"', *American Literary History,*

Vol. 26, No. 2, Oxford University Press, (Summer, 2014), pp. 339-346

Lawson Richard, 'The Brutal Beauty of "12 Years a Slave"', *The Atlantic Daily, Culture,* Sept.16, 2013, at www.theatlantic.com/culture/archive/2013/09/12 (20/02/23)

 Northup Solomon, *Twelve Years a Slave: The Black History Classic,* (Wiley and Sons, July 2021)

Stauffer John, '12 Years between Life and Death', *American Literary History, Vol. 26, No. 2, Oxford University Press,* (Summer 2014)

<u>Women's Roles in Shakespearean plays Macbeth and Othello</u>

Shakespeare William, 'Othello' in Jonathan Bate and Eric Rasmussen (ed.), The RSC Shakespeare, Macmillan, (2009)
Shakespeare William, 'The Tragedy of Macbeth, at http://shakespeare.mit.edu/macbeth/full.html

<u>Great Writers of American Literature, their influence and powerful words!</u>

 Culp Beth Mary, 'Religion in the poetry of Langston Hughes', Phylon (1960-), 3rd Quarter., Vol 48 no 3, Clarke Atlanta University, pp 240-245

Emanuel A James, 'The Christ and the killers', Langston Hughes: Twayne's United States Authors series 123, (Gale 1967 New York), pp 89-118

Emerson Waldo Ralph, 'Nature', in Robert S. Levine (9th ed.), The Norton anthology of American literature 1820-1865, Volume B, (New York, 2017)

Flashpointmag.com/hughes_scottsbro_christ.htm

Hughes Langston, in Robert S. Levine (9th ed.), The Norton anthology of American literature, 1914-1945 Vol D, (New York 2017)

Ramos Peter, 'In and out of the game: Whitman's politics, poetry and better self', CEA Critic vol 71 no 1, The John's Hopkins University Press, (Fall 2008), pp 27-44

Whitman Walt, 'Preface to leaves of grass', in Robert S. Levine (9th ed.), The Norton anthology of American literature 1820-1865, Volume B, (New York, 2017)

Whitman Walt, 'The Sleepers', in Robert S. Levine (9th ed.), The Norton Anthology of American Literature 1820-1865, Volume B, (New York, 2017

Whitman Walt, 'Leaves of Grass', Dover Thrift edition, (2007)

www.poetryfoundation.org/poems

How are Gender and Sexuality explored in the literary work of "Frankisstein: A Love Story" by Jeanette Winterson

Allardice Lisa. "*Interview Jeanette Winterson: I did worry about looking at sexbots*". The Guardian. [2019].

Corr – Thomas Johanna. *"Frankissstein by Jeanette Winterson: Review an inventive reanimation"*. The Guardian. [2019].

Milne Pamela. *"Genesis from Eve's point of view"*. Washington Post. [26/3/1989].

Hayasaki Erika. "Is AI Sexist". [16/01/2017]. < http://foreignpolicy.com/2017/01/16/women-vs-the-machine/>.

Scholes Lucy. *"Bodies of work: Jeanette Winterson stitches together two stories inspired by the birth of Mary Shelley's literary monster"*. The Scotsman. Edinburgh. [06/2019].

Smith Llewellyn Julia. *"I always knew I was brilliant. The booker took a while to catch up: Jeanette Winterson has finally made it onto"*. Sunday Times. London. [29/07/2019].

Winterson Jeanette. *"Frankisssten: A Love story"*. Penguin/Vintage, Jonathan Cape, [2019].

<u>Jane Austen's use of irony in Pride and Prejudice forces readers to make alliances with some characters over others.</u>

Austen, Jane. *Pride and Prejudice.* Donald Gray, Mary A. Favret (4th ed.), Norton Company, New York 2016.

Ewin, E.R. "Pride Prejudice and shyness". *Philosophy* 65. 252. 1990: 137–154.

Fraiman, Susan. "The Humiliation of Elizabeth Bennet". *Unbecoming Women.* Columbia University Press (New York 1993):59-87

Rytting, Rebecca, Jenny. "Jane Austen meets Carl Jung: Pride, Prejudice and Personality Theory". *Jane Austen Society of North America* 22. 1. (2001)

Sherrod, Barbara. "Pride and Prejudice: A Classic Love Story". *Jane Austen Society of North America.* Persuasions #11, (Fort Collins 1989):66-69

Sorbo, Nedregotten, Maire. "Interpretation of Jane Austen's Irony on Screen and in Translation: A Comparison of Some Samples". *Women's Writing Journal Elizabeth to Victorian Period.* 2018: 525 – 535

Tanner, Tony. "Jane Austen: Knowledge and Opinion: Pride and Prejudice". *Harvard University Press.* (Cambridge, Massachusetts 1986)

Slavery and Dehumaninastion through Literary Work

 Alberti John, 'The Nigger Huck: Race, Identity, and the Teaching of Huckleberry Finn', College English, Vol. 57, No. 8, National Council of Teachers of English, (Dec. 1995

Silko Marmon Lesile, 'Ceremony', Penguin Random House, (UK, 2020)

Twain Mark, 'The Adventures of Huckleberry Finn', Collins Classics, Harper Press, (2013)

Self-Reliance through Literature

Emerson Waldo Ralf, 'Self Reliance', Robert S Levine (9th ed.), *Norton Anthology American Literature 1820-1865,*

Franziska Justyna, 'Individualism and the spirit of America', *Emerson goes to the movies: Individualism Walt Disney Company's Post 1989 Aminated Films,* (Cambridge 2014), pp 13-34

Griffis B Rachel, 'Reformation leads to self-reliance: The Protestantism of Transcendentalism', *Department of Language and Literature* (Sterling College USA 21/2/2017)

Msabah A Barnabe, 'Refugee migrants as agents of change: Strategies or improved livelihoods and self-reliance', *Verbum et Ecclesia Vol 40 issue 1* (African Christian University Kenya 2/2019)

Ruetenik Tadd, 'Self Reliance plagiarism and the suicide of imitation', *Teaching American Literature: A journal of theory and practise Vol 8 issue 1*, (St Ambrose University, Spring 2015), pp70-80

<u>Feminism with Ngozi Adichie is seen through Beyonce's Song Flawless.</u>

Beyoncé – flawless ft. Chimamanda Ngozi Adichie , YouTube

Bianco's Marcie, 'Chimamanda Ngozi Adichie and Beyoncé: Feminism in action', WMC news and features: arts and culture, (Oct 12, 2016) at http://womensmediacenter.com

Ferguson Sian, 'Privilege 101: A quick guide and dirty guide', *Everyday feminism* (Sept. 29, 2014), at http://everydayfeminism.com/author/sianferguson

Flawless, 'Lyrics by Beyonce', *Lyrics on demand* at www.lyricsondemand.com/b/beyonceknowleslyrics/flawleslyrics.html

Greer Germaine, *The Female Eunuch*, Harper Perennial Classics,

Jenainati Cathia, Graves Judy and Milton Jem, *Feminism A Graphic Guide*, (Canada 2019)

McIntosh Peggy, 'white privilege unpacking the invisible knapsack', L Ayu Saraswati, Barbara Shaw & Heather Rellihan (ed.), Introduction to women's gender and sexuality studies: Interdisciplinary and Intersectional approaches, (1988)

<u>Perception of Race through Robin Diangelo's Work</u>

Diangelo Robin, 'White fragility: Why it is so hard for white people to talk about Racism', *Allen Lane, Penguin Random House*, (UK 2019), pp15-69

<u>A life of independence through James Joyce's work 'A Portrait of the Young Artist as a Young Man'</u>

Azizmohammadi Fatemeh and Kamarzade Sepide, 'Study of Stephen Dedalus the man protagonist of A Portrait of the Artist as a Young Man', *Advances in language and literary studies, vol 5 no 2 (Australia April 2014)*

Farrell Kevin, 'The reverend Stephen Dedalus, S.J.: Sacramental structure in A Portrait of the Artist as a Young Man, *James Joyce Quarterly, vol 49 no 1, university of Tulsa* (Fall 2011), pp 27-40

Jones P. S. Robert, 'Language form and emotion in James Joyce's A Portrait of the Artist as a Young Man: A Literary Analysis', *Advance in Language and Literary Studies Vol 8 issue 5, Bangor University, (Bangor 2017)*

Joyce James, 'A Portrait of the Artist as a Young Man', *Penguin Books*, (1996)

Khan Ali Sajjad, 'The politics of the romantic aesthetics: Fromm James Joyce's Stephen Hero to A Portrait of the Artist as a Young Man', *Journal of the Research Society of Pakistan, vol 57, issue 2, (Lahore Dec 2020)*

Ross Stephen and Yazdani Saeed, 'Carl Rogers notion of self-actualisation in Joyce's A Portrait of the Artist as a Young Man', 3L: the Southeast Asian journal of English language studies, vol 25, no 2, pp 61-73

Simion Otillia Minodora, 'Modernist techniques in a Portrait of the Artist as a Young Man by James Joyce',

Annals of the Constantin Brancusi letter and social science series, issue 4, university of Targu Jiu, (2013)

Structural Racism in Toni Morrison's book "Beloved"

Day Lannette, 'Identity Formation and White Presence in Toni Morrison's Beloved and the Bluest Eye', *McKendree University, Issue 17, (Summer2011)*

Humann Duerre Heather, 'Bigotry, Breast Milk, Bric-a-Brac, a Baby, and a bit in "Beloved": Toni Morrison's Portrayal of Racism and Hegemony', *Interdisciplinary Literary Studies, Vol. 6, No. 1, Penn State University, (Fall, 2004)*

Morrison Toni, 'Beloved' *Vintage Classics (London, 2007)*

Primlyn Linda A, 'The Concept Of Blackness in Toni Morrison's Beloved', *Indian Review of World Literature in English, Vol. 8, No. 2, (July 2012)*

Rani Anjo Dr., The Portrayal of Slavery in Toni Morrison's Beloved', *International Journal of Creative Research thoughts, Vol. 10, Issue 2 (February 2022)*

Rashid Amina, Rana Masud Md., 'Racial Inequality and Sexist Oppression in Toni Morrison's Beloved', *Language Literacy: Journal of Linguistics Literature and Language Teaching, Vol. 5, No. 1, (June 2011)*

Thohiriyah T, 'Solidifying The White Domination through Racism and Slavery in Toni Morrison's Beloved', *Language Circle: Journal of Language and Literature. Vol. 14, No. 1, (October, 2019)*

Zamalin Alex, 'Beloved Citizens: Toni Morrison's "Beloved", Racial Inequality and American Public Policy', *Women's Studies Quarterly, Vol.42, No.1/2, The feminist Press University of New York, (Spring/Summer, 2014)*

Charles Dickens Oliver Twist, of the criminal underworld and its relation to legitimate society.

Dickens Charles, 'Oliver Twist, *illustrated edition Wordsworth Classics, (2000)*

Michael Steven, 'Criminal Slang in "Oliver Twist": Dickens Survival Code', *Style, Language, Grammar, Prosody, Vol. 27, No. 1 Peen State University Press (Spring, 1993)*

Samples N. Megan, 'This World of Sorrow and Troubles: The Criminal Type of Oliver Twist, *Georgia State University, (2013)*

Sirabian Robert, 'The illusion of Game Playing in Oliver Twist, *CEA Critic, Vol. 79, No. 1, John Hopkins University Press, (March 2017)*

Human Desire through Milton's Paradise Lost

Dohal H Gussim, 'Humanising Satan of Milton's Paradise Lost', *Theory and Practice in Language Studies, Vol 12, No 5* (May 2022)

Marcus S Leah, ' Ecocriticism and vitalism in Paradise Lost, *Milton Quarterly Vol. 49, No. 2, Wiley* (May 2015), pp96-111 at p 96

Milton John, 'Paradise Lost & Paradise Regained', Signet Classics, (2010)

Sublime Through The French Revolution

Burke Edmund, 'Reflections On The Revolution In France', *Oxford World Classics, OPU Oxford: Reissue edition (26 March 2009)*

Butler Marilyn, 'Telling it Like A Story: The French Revolution as Narrative', *English Romanticism and the French Revolution, Studies in Romanticism, Vol. 28, No. 3, (Fall, 1989)*

Dickens Charles, 'A Tale Of Two Cities, *Oxford World Classics, OPU Oxford: Reissue Edition, (May 2008)*

Huet Helene- Maire, 'The Revolutionary Sublime', *Eighteenth-Century Studies, Vol 28, No. 1, John Hopkins University Press, (Autumn. 1994)*

Mahmood A. Karzan, 'The Sublime: Edmund Burke on the French Revolution, *Journal of Humanities and Social Sciences, Vol.4, No.1, Koya University, (June 2021)*,

Maniquis M Robert, 'Filling Up and Emptying The Sublime: Terror in British Radical Culture', *Huntington Library Quarterly, British Radical Culture of the 1970s, Vol 63, No 3, University of Pennsylvania Press, (2000)*

Oladjehou B. Barnabe Dr, ' Charles Dickens analysis of the French Revolution in a Tale Of Two Cities: A Critical Study, *International Journal of Humanities, Social Sciences and Education, Vol 4, Issue 4, (April 2017)*

Shelley Bysshe Percy, 'The Masque Of Anarchy', *Ragged Hand, Read and Co., (2020)*

Women's History through Radio Podcasts – By Ashling McGee

Baker Patricia, 'The Troublesome Nun', *Ground Breakers, Newstalk*

Baker Patricia, 'Egg Money', *Documentary on Newstalk*

Baker Patricia, ' Do Disturb' *Documentary on Newstalk*

Breathnach Declan, 'Modern Slavery is Going On Right Under Our Noses', *The Irish Times, Wednesday, November 13 (2019)*

Dowd O'Mary, 'Margaret MacCurtain (1929-2020): an appreciation, *Irish historical Studies, Special Issue 170: A New Agenda for Women's and Gender History in Ireland, Vol 46, Queens University Belfast, (November 2022)*

Obituaries, 'Mamo McDonald Obituary: A pioneering 'born again' Irish feminist', *Irish Times, Thursday 24, (2021)*

Walsh Fionnuala, 'The Troublesome Nun', *Reviews, NewsTalk, 3 & 9 October 28 December 2021, Issue 2, Volume 30, (March/April 2022)*

Gender Relations throughout Early Modern Europe

Bogucka Maria, 'Phases of Women's Lives', *Women in Early Modern Polish Society against the European Background*, Taylor and Francis Group (28/07/04)

Hanks – Wiesner E Merry, 'Individuals in Society 1450-1600', *Early Modern Europe, (2nd Ed.)*, Cambridge University Press, (2013)

Hanks – Wiesner E Merry, 'Royal Ordinance regarding inheritance, Portugal 16th Century', *Chapter two: Individuals in Society 1450-1600, Primary source Chapter 2, No 4*, Cambridge university press, (2013) at WWW.Cambridge.org/wiesnerhanks

Kreps Barbara, 'The Paradox of Women: The legal position of Early Modern Wives and Thomas Dekker's "The Honest Whore"', *ELH, Spring, Vol 69, No 2*, John Hopkins university press,(Spring 2002)

Pihl Christopher, 'Gender and Labour and State Formation in 16th Century Sweden', *The historical journal, Vol 58, No 3,* Cambridge University Press, (Uppsala University, 2015)

Poska M Allyson, 'The Case for Agentic Gender Norms for Women in Early Modern Europe', *Gender and History, vol 30, No 2,* John Wiley and Sons Ltd.,(July 2018)

 Warner Lydan, 'The Dignity and Misery of Men… and Women', *The Ideas of man and woman in Renaissance France: Print, Rhetoric and Law*, Taylor and Francis Group, (28-03-11).

<u>Vagrancy in Ireland in 1822-23</u>

Archbishop of Tuam, 'Evidence of His Grace the Archbishop of Tuam', *Appendix to the first report from the commissioners for inquiring into the state of the classes in Ireland* (Tuam, 2006)

Collins Mr, 'person who attended the examination', *Appendix to the first report from the commissioners for inquiring into the state of the classes in Ireland,* (Mayo,2006)

Corbat John, 'person who attended the examination', *Appendix to the first report from the commissioners for inquiring into the state of the classes in Ireland,* (2006)

Kelly John, 'person who attended the examination', *Appendix to the first report from the commissioners for inquiring into the state of the classes in Ireland,* (2006)

Significant Mr, 'person who attended the examination', *Appendix to the first report from the commissioners for inquiring into the state of the classes in Ireland* (Mayo,2006)

McHale Dr. 'Evidence of Dr McHale, Roman Catholic Archbishop of Tuam, Appendix to the first report from the commissioners for inquiring into the state of the classes in Ireland, (2006)

McNally Edward, 'person who attended the examination', *Appendix to the first report from the commissioners for inquiring into the state of the classes in Ireland* (Mayo,2006)

Mullin Anthony, 'person who attended the examination', *Appendix to the first report from the commissioners for inquiring into the state of the classes in Ireland,* (2006)

White Michael, 'person who attended the examination', *Appendix to the first report from the commissioners for inquiring into the state of the classes in Ireland* (Omagh, Galway, 2006)

<u>Developments from the 19th Century shaped Ireland into today's society</u>

Bielenberg Andy, 'The Irish brewery industry and the rise of Guinness 1790-1914', in Terry Gourvish, Richard G Wilson (ed.), *The dynamics of the modern brewery industry, Taylor and Francis group*, (1998)

Delay Cara, 'The devotional revolution on the local level: Parish life in post-famine Ireland', *U.S Catholic historian Ireland and America: Religious political and social movements, vol 22 no 3,* (catholic university press America, summer 2004)

Foster F. R., *Modern Ireland 1600-1972,* Penguin Books (1989)

Gray Peter, *The Irish Famine, Thames and Hudson, New Horizons, (London, 1995)*

Johnson H James, 'The context of migration: the example of Ireland in 19th century', *Transactions of the Institute of British Geographers, vol 15 no 3* (1990)

Larkin Emmet, 'The devotional revolution in Ireland 1850-75', *The American historical review, vol 77 no 3, Oxford university press*, (June 1972)

Lee J, 'Money and beer in Ireland 1790-1875', *The economic history review, vol 19 no 1, New series*, (1966)

Nally David, 'That coming storm: The Irish poor law, colonial biopolitics, and the great famine', *Annals of the Association of American Geographers, vol 98 no 3*, (2008)

Powderly G William, 'How infection shaped history: Lessons from the Irish Famine', *Transactions of the American Clinical and Climatological Association, Vol 130*, (2019)

Uneke Okori, 'Troubled Geographies: A spatial history of religion and society in Ireland', *International source science review, Issue 2 Vol 91*, (2015)

Rushdie's 'Midnight's Children' The Human Relations Through Life of India

Hashmat Shaheen, 'Rushdie's Midnights Children and the Legacy of Partition at http://www.shaheenhasmat.com/essays/rushdie's-midnight's-children-and-the-legacy-of-partition/

Hogan Colm Patrick, 'Midnights Children: Kashmir and the politics of identity', *Twentieth-century literature, Vol. 47 No. 4, Duke University Press*, (Winter, 2001), pp 510-544 at pp 530 -531

Rushdie Saleem, 'Midnights Children', *Penguin Random House, Vintage Classics*, (2021)

George Orwell's essay 'Shooting an Elephant' By Ashling McGee

Orwell George *"Shooting an Elephant"*. George Orwell's essays and articles, Penguin, (1936)

Imagination and Memory of Life through Whitman and Silko

Babaienia Leila, 'In Between History and Memory: Leslie Marmon Silko's Fictional World', *Critical Literature Studies, Vol. iv, No.2, Series 8, (Spring/Summer 2022)*

Buck E Neal, 'Whitman in the Waves', *Literary Imagination, Vol. 15, issue 3, (Nov. 2013)*

Levine S. Robert, 'Walt Whitman', *The Norton Anthology American Literature 1820-1865, Volume B, Ninth edition (2017)*

Orvell Miles, 'Whitman's Transformed Eye' *The Real Thing: Imitation and Authenticity, American Culture, University of North Carolina Press, (1999)*

Silko, 'Language and Literature from a Pueblo Indian Perspective', *English Literature: Opening up the Canon, (1981)*

Sturken Marita and Lisa Cartwright, Chapter 1 Images, Power, and Politics, *From practices of looking: An Introduction to visual culture, (OUP, 2009)*

Whitman Walt, 'Leaves of Grass, *The original 1855 edition, Dover Thrift Editions, (New York, 2007)*

Renewal and Rebirth through Sylvia Plath's poem The Elm

Fremaux Anne, ' For a Critical Theory of the Anthropocene', *institute for Interdisciplinary Research into the*

Anthropocene, at http://iiraorg.com/2019/09/01/for-a-critical-theory-of-the-anthropocene/

Plumwood Val,' Nature Self and Gender: Feminism Environmental Philosophy and the Critique of Rationalism', *Hypatia, Vol.6, No. 1, Ecological Feminism,* (Spring, 1991)

Plumwood Val, 'Introduction' in *Feminism and the Mastery of Nature, Taylor and Francis e-library,* (2003)

Thompson Charis, 'Back to Nature?', *Isis, Vol. 97, No. 3, University of Chicago Press,* (September 2006)

Zhang Xiaohong, 'An ecofeminist perspective on Sylvia Plath and Zhai Yongming', *Comparative Literature Studies, Vol. 55, No. 4, Penn State University Press,* (2018),

Danez Smith's poem 'Dear White America' and racial injustice

Cunningham Vinson, 'The Argument of Afropessimism', *The New Yorker, July 20, Issue 2020,* at www.newyorker.com/magazine/2020/07/20/the-argument-of-afro pessimism (29. Oct.)

Roberts Dorothy, 'Torture and the Biopolitics of Race,' *University of Miami Law Review, Vol 6, No 229,* (2008)

Roberts Dorothy, 'White Privilege and the Biopolitics of Race, in Kirkland and Ellis Professor, *Understanding and Dismantling Privilege, North-western University School of Law, Vol 1, Issue 1,* (2010),

Weir Sebastian, 'Consider Afro – Pessimism', *American Studies, Vol 59, No3,* Universitatsverlag Winter Gmbh, (2014)

Wilderson B. Frank. III, 'Social Death and Narrative Aporia in 12 Years a Slave, Black Camera, Vol 7, No 1, Indiana University Press, (Fall, 2015),

Milton's Paradise Lost

Lieb Michael, 'How Stanley Fish works: How Milton works by Stanley Fish,' *The Journal of Religion, Vol.82, No.2,* University of Chicago Press, (April 2002)

Milton John, 'Paradise Lost and Paradise Regained,' *Signet Classics*, (Nov. 2010)

Nafi Ismail Subhi Jamal Dr., 'A Critical analysis of Milton's Poetic style as revealed in his epic poem Paradise Lost Book I And II,' *Research Journal of English Language and Literature, Vol.4, Issue 1,* Al-Quds University (Jan. – Mar. 2016)

Wheeler Thomas, 'Milton's Blank Verse Couplets,' *The Journal of English and Germanic Philology, Vol.66, No.3*, University of Illinois, (Jul. 1967)

Wilson, Robert F., 'Paradise Lost II. 310 -416: Beelzebub's Satanic Solution', *CEA Critic, Vol.37, No.2,* The John Hopkins University Press, (January 1975)

Photo analysis of Bill Hudson's photo of 'The Civil Rights Movement

McWhorter Diane, 'Carry Me Home: Birmingham, Alabama: The climate battle of the civil rights Revolution', *Simon & Schuster, New York (2001)*

Shipler K David, 'Bombingham Revisited', www.nytimes.com, (March 18, 2001)

Tuck Steven, 'We Ain't What We Ought To Be', *Belknap Press, Harvard University Press, Cambridge, Massachusetts, London, England,* (2010)

Seeing Life Through Different Lenses
Ashling McGee

www.ingramcontent.com/pod-product-compliance
Lightning Source LLC
Chambersburg PA
CBHW071919150726
47999CB00001B/41